HOW TO SUFFER OUTSIDE

HOW TO SUFFER OUTSIDE

A Beginner's Guide to Hiking and Backpacking

DIANA HELMUTH

Illustrations by Latasha Dunston

MOUNTAINEERS
BOOKS

MOUNTAINEERS BOOKS is dedicated to
the exploration, preservation, and enjoyment
of outdoor and wilderness areas.

1001 SW Klickitat Way, Suite 201, Seattle, WA 98134
800-553-4453, www.mountaineersbooks.org

Printed in China
Distributed in the United Kingdom by Cordee, www.cordee.co.uk
26 25 24 23   3 4 5 6 7

Copyeditor: Laura Lancaster
Design and layout: Jen Grable
Illustrator: Latasha Dunston

Library of Congress Cataloging-in-Publication Data for this title is on file at https://lccn.loc .gov/2021008626. The LC ebook record is available at https://lccn.loc.gov/2021008627.

Mountaineers Books titles may be purchased for corporate, educational, or other promotional sales, and our authors are available for a wide range of events. For information on special discounts or booking an author, contact our customer service at 800-553-4453 or mbooks@ mountaineersbooks.org.

Printed on FSC®-certified materials

ISBN (paperback): 978-1-68051-311-0
ISBN (ebook): 978-1-68051-312-7

An independent nonprofit publisher since 1960

To my mother—
who first called me "peanut hiker,"
handed me banana chips,
and told me there was a surprise
at the top of the mountain

CONTENTS

PREFACE

WELCOME. In your hands, you are holding a book about backpacking written by a nonprofessional backpacker. (Is professional backpacking a thing? I don't even know. Hmm. That, that right there should explain my qualifications nicely.)

More specifically, this book by a nonprofessional backpacker is for aspiring nonprofessional backpackers. You know, people who spend ten hours a month copying photoshopped images of sugar-dusted mountains and sun-dappled redwood glades onto a Pinterest board called "Wanderlust." Yeah. Welcome. We're gonna do it. We're gonna get you out there.

The purpose of this preface is both to welcome you and to absolve myself of any legal liability for potentially killing you. Let's be clear: I am not the *Man vs. Wild* guy, Tom Brown Jr., or someone who's ever spent 127 hours debating whether to cut off their own arm. Also, I'm sorry if someone got this for you because they thought it was the Cheryl Strayed book; I am unfortunately not Cheryl Strayed. I am an administrative assistant who sits in an IKEA chair all day and gets upset when people don't color-code their spreadsheet columns correctly. I have a bunion and I eat too much cake. I am, without question, unqualified to be giving you advice about survival in nature. Mostly.

What I am is what I assume you are: someone who saw a pretty picture of a mountain, and then thought it might be a nice idea to take 70,000 footsteps to say you saw it in person. If I can do it, and not only survive, but enjoy it so much I do it again and again, you probably can too.

Contrary to the examples that most blogs, magazines, and brand-name catalogs feature, a backpacking hobby doesn't have to be expensive, extremely arduous, or put on hold until you are at your goal weight. There's an optimal way to backpack, and then there's the "probably good enough" way. You are reading about the latter.

The advice in this book comes from lessons I learned in the literal field, wisdom passed down to me by patient, loving teachers, books published a couple decades ago that have stood the test of time, and a few panicked Google sessions ten hours before a flight. So far, it has all worked well enough. (I'm alive, aren't I?)

But my advice is necessarily imperfect, both because I am not an expert and because, frankly, there is no one right way to backpack. A few adages are universally agreed upon ("cotton kills," for example), but as new technology rolls out, many topics are hotly debated (such as whether to trust the GPS app on your smartphone over a dedicated device or if the long-term health effects of DEET are worse than the mosquitoes it saves you from). There is no central authority in backpacking; we have no papacy, no organized decision-making structure, and aside from the occasional REI swap meet, there aren't any official gatherings. Instead, there's just some combination of what you read about someone else doing, what your teacher/dad/mom taught you, and the instructions that came with that pump-socket-thing you bought online last Black Friday.

I'm assuming you picked up this book because you've heard the call of the wild (or a friend gave it to you, because they think you've heard the call of the wild). Maybe you've already dabbled a bit in the great outdoors. Maybe someone took you fishing at a high-elevation lake when you were eight years old, and you find yourself drawn to the memory of breathing crisp, alien air in a valley of deafening quiet. Maybe you borrowed a mini-van from your BFF's mom in high school and corralled a group of friends into "camping" (i.e., you all got very drunk on Tecate in an open field and one of you tripped in the fire). Or, maybe you have even been on an over-night hiking trip. Maybe you own a mummy sleeping bag, a sleeping pad, and some stuff sacks.

Whatever your history, you've tasted enough of the wilderness to know you want a bigger bite. You've melted into a golden sunset, felt the wind rush up your body on the edge of a cliff, and felt your eyes stretch into white circles in the face of a moonrise. You understand there are places in the world so fucking beautiful that even emotionally stunted men living in the mid-nineteenth century whose siblings died from famine and pox were driven to write ecstatic poetry and perform acts of religious fervor in their presence. You are itching to go see them. You aren't scared of walking a couple miles. You are pretty sure you own a knife, even if you can't remember where it is. You feel ready, even though you're not quite sure for what.

Let's talk about that last part for a minute—that nagging question: *Why . . . do I want to go backpacking?*

Backpacking is an eight-hour leg day that ends with no shower, a sunburn, and sleeping on the ground. It's not so much about seeing whether you can survive without Grubhub or Netflix or FaceTime. It's about going somewhere where you won't be able to FaceTime anyone even if you think you're about to die. So why the hell do you want to do this?

Some people believe this is a personal, mystical question: "Why did I climb the mountain? Because it was there." This is the iconic response coined by George Mallory, which imagines nature as some ineffable, majestic plane of existence, and to define it is to tarnish its magnetism. The question cannot have an answer; the wild that can be named is not the eternal wild.

I think this is bullshit, and I have an answer. You long to go into nature because, unlike your home, job, car, bed, or school, it's quiet, really quiet— the kind of quiet that exists when there is nothing to turn on. But this is deeper than "unplugging" from the attention economy that has been steadily eroding your attention span since the first iPhone came out. You long to go into nature because nature doesn't care about you. To be clear, it's not that nature sees you, accepts you for who you are, and loves you anyway: nature just doesn't give a shit about you.

Someday, at some point in your life (if it hasn't happened already), you're going to look in the mirror and see something misshapen. A pile of failed goals, a bulging heap of inadequacy, one solitary, tragic hillock of human flesh. You'll have no idea how anyone ever loved you, or will ever love you, or how you will ever accomplish anything worth remembering. You won't see yourself. You won't even see a person. You'll see only a broken promise.

This is the best time to put everything in a backpack and leave. Why? Because nature doesn't care that you feel this way. It doesn't care about your job, your kids, your career goals, your half-baked plan to go back to school and get your masters, or your failed attempts at the Whole30 diet. Nature doesn't care if you've read *Twilight* or Tolstoy, if you married the right person, or if you're a bad person because you stopped speaking to your dad.

In nature, everything is distinctly *not* about you. Wake up—no one cares. Eat breakfast—no one cares. Pack up your shit—no one cares. Start walking—no one cares. If anything goes wrong, and you need help, or a hug—no one cares. You cannot call your bestie or look up your ex on Facebook to imagine what it would be like if they were there with you. With every step you take, the insignificance of your problems in the face of the natural world will be unavoidable. No one will be there to care about you—except you. In other words, you will be forced to self-soothe.

Your desire to go into nature comes from the same part of you that wishes to be secure. It doesn't want to depend on others for self-assurance and approval. It doesn't want to be addicted to buzzing rectangles and 30-second videos and 280-character quips. It craves reflection and depth and connection with a more tangible, eternal whole. It wants to give you a minute to work out all the tangled crap in your brain that you've been avoiding. (Don't pretend you're not doing this. You know you can't even take a shit without checking Instagram.)

As the world becomes wonderfully, unavoidably digitized, all things branded as "returning to nature"—hiking, camping, farmsteading—are becoming increasingly trendy (in the West, at least). This has been happening for a few decades, but it feels like it's reaching a bit of a fever pitch, doesn't it? This uptick is good (nature may not care, but I do). In addition to reclaiming a way of life we're afraid we're forgetting, nature-focused hobbies teach us emotional relativity, self-reliance, and confidence. These are lessons we are somewhat missing in our domesticated, supply-chain-dependent, overtalkative world—a world that evolution did not prepare us for and that, despite all its amenities, appears ready to fail us at the drop of a hat (or a virus).

Backpacking, however, is not the most approachable hobby. I still barely feel like I belong here. That's why this book exists. Insofar as I can, I want to help you navigate the landscape of expensive gear, specialized maps, and apparent disregard for human life. Getting started can be daunting or feel as if it's reserved for either street-smart, train-hopping hippies or statuesque, upper-middle-class white people and their organically fed children.

Rest assured, though, that backpacking is for you, if you want it. If you can walk, put stuff in a bag, and remember to eat, you can backpack. It's called returning to nature for a reason: for eons, we lived in it exclusively. (And it killed us—a lot. But now we have iodine and boxed mac 'n cheese, so your odds are way up.) The outdoors is still there, waiting for you.

If you go backpacking, you are going to get broken down, and then built back up again into . . . well, whatever you are when you're not trying to impress anyone but yourself. Are you ready to find out who that is? Let's begin. (Warning: You're going to shit in a bag.)

Chapter 1

INTRODUCTIONS
Who Am I, and Why Do I Believe in You?

"The complications of unnecessary systems are about to melt away."
  —A backpacking expert

There are plenty of jokes about backpackers: "Wait, you sleep outside by *choice*?" "So, you're paying to act like you're homeless?" "F&*#%!g white people." All these jokes are fair and correct.[1]

Some people will tell you, both directly and indirectly, that backpacking is for young, white individuals at the peak of their physical prowess, who are so financially secure they can take two months off work to "find themselves" among the trees and run up astronomical bills on a suburban garage's worth of specialized equipment. They own a $2,000 doohickey for absolutely every single task that can or will take place in nature, and they can't wait to tell you about how revolutionary it is. On the other end of the

---

1. Well, except for the homeless thing. Choice is the major difference, of course, but there's also a far higher incidence of German tourists.

backpacker-stereotype spectrum are the minimalists: earth-worshipping power hippies who cut the straps off their backpacks, shun the constant bombardment of newfangled gadgetry from the Wilderness Industrial Complex™, and jump at any opportunity to tell you (but almost never teach you) how they can start a fire with nothing more than a vintage tin can opener and a nugget of deer poop.

Let me be the first to offer my hand and tell you that all of this is bullshit. You don't have to be either of these people. Regardless of where you come from, nature is a great equalizer, and people walk into the woods for hundreds of reasons—from getting off drugs to fulfilling fitness goals to reconnecting with the natural world. The rules of backpacking have nothing do with how much money you have, what you look like, or whether you can afford to take two days or two weeks off for an adventure.

Yes, you do need a little cash to get your gear pile started, but it's not as bad as you'd think. Going outside is not the hobby equivalent of shopping at Whole Foods—we can't all afford $10.99/lb. radicchio, but we can all access the sky.

———

I WAS FIRST INTRODUCED TO backpacking by my mom, an ex-commune Christian ER nurse and single parent of three daughters who has spent most of her fifties and sixties being hotter than I was at nineteen. She currently lives in an ancient Victorian outside of California's wine country, home-brewing cold remedies from the herbs in her garden, and occasionally adopting stray chickens. My mom claims she got into backpacking late in life, but for as long as I can remember, if she had a day off, she was out of the house and on a hike. For most of 2001 she was climbing the Himalayas, and she spent half of 2004 wandering around Indonesia. By the time I was in college, she was knee-deep into Tom Brown Jr.'s Cherokee-inspired tracker courses, and eventually walked into Desolation Wilderness—a 63,960-acre stretch of NorCal wildland known for freezing water, bears, and sharp rocks—carrying only a knife and a bag of trail mix ("just to see what would happen").[2]

———

2. To be clear, that's not backpacking—that's menopause.

My mom took me on my first backpacking trip when I was fifteen. We went to the California classic: Yosemite National Park, where I saw the sunny, summer waves of Tuolumne Meadows, discovered what it felt like to walk all day with only the sky for a clock, and learned how to deal with the blisters I inevitably got on my feet. The weekend ended well: I'd slept through a rainstorm, learned the importance of washing DEET off your hands before using a tampon, and proudly shrouded four of my own blisters in moleskin. However, this trip was simply a generous tutorial. My mom was preparing me for a larger event that autumn, an experience that would become the basis for all my future backpacking knowledge: Team.

The Team Program is an experiential academic and outdoor high school learning program that plucks twenty-four willing students from across Marin County (the yuppie utopia north of San Francisco) out of their regularly scheduled junior year and drops them off in front of two teachers, a single room, and no bells. The two teachers in charge were Chuck Ford and Patchen Homitz. Chuck was a grizzled, mad-professor-looking papa in his sixties with an affinity for Spam products who first described himself to his students as "a former postal worker who believes you should turn in your homework on time." Patchen was a mountain-biking bro in his forties with a military haircut, a Bill Bryson book tucked under one arm, and a saintly tolerance for his students referring to him, to his face, as "Patchy-Poo."

In addition to the quality programming you'd get at any other school (history, social studies, math, and English), Chuck and Patchen taught us things like wilderness medicine, backcountry navigation, financial literacy, and career preparedness. We calculated how large a mortgage we could afford with the average salary of our dream job and practiced our first-aid skills on screaming actors covered in fake blood in the school kitchen. On Tuesdays, we volunteered at a charity of our choice.

The main events at Team, however, were three multiday backpacking trips in California: one to the Yosemite Wilderness, another to Joshua Tree National Park, and a third to Mount Shasta. (Summiting that 14,000-foot glaciated volcano served as a "you did it!" metaphor for the end of the year.)

Aside from my mother, Chuck and Patchen taught me nearly every-thing I know about backpacking. In fact, the majority of this book is based on their teachings. Mind you, neither one of them told us anything about zero-degree down sleeping quilts or the latest designs in ultralight bidet bottles. At Team, we borrowed all our gear from the school's gigantic store-room of heavy, lovingly used sleeping bags, stoves, and fleece pants. But they did show us how to use all of it—and above all, how to think about it.

When I tell people about Team, it sounds like some kind of expen-sive rehab program for troubled youth. They assume I must have been a self-harming, oxy-addicted terror of a teenager, blasting Tool out of my room at two in the morning. My hapless, power-suit-wearing parents, cursed with more money than time to discipline me, would have had no choice but to send me away to this tough-love hippie boot camp. Granted, Team was kind of a mix of Outward Bound and independent study, two programs unrighteously branded as being for "troubled teens," but nothing could be further from the truth about my relationship with it.

I was a very good kid in high school. I got straight As. I made green smoothies for breakfast. I was such a reliable non-drug-doer that my friends would have me store their weed so their parents wouldn't find it. The first person who got me drunk was my own mother after she acciden-tally handed me the wrong juice glass at a party when I was sixteen. I had friends, belonged to the drama club, went to dance class after school. I was a "good kid."

But like a lot of teenagers, I think I was a little depressed. I was at a crossroads of pressures where everyone was telling me I could be what-ever I wanted, which made me lucky, but I had no idea how to pull any of it off, which meant I was bad.

Team offered solace to kids at that crossroads. Most of us who applied to the program, myself included, did so not because we explicitly wanted to strap ninety pounds to our backs and walk uphill. (That one guy who applied because he had been leading river-rafting trips since age four-teen or whatever doesn't count.) We applied because we were already struggling under the weight of expectations of feeling like the college we got into would determine our starting position in the hierarchy of life, and the back-crushing amount of homework to get there (not to mention the fear-to-benefit ratio of thousands of dollars of student debt). Then of course there was the ever-present temptation to check out and crawl under the warm gray blanket of apathy with some NyQuil or a stolen bottle of Vicodin. I wanted to check out of my life. But I didn't want to check out of my future—Team felt like a secret third option for going forward without burning out. (Plus, maybe they'd also teach me to wrestle a bear—what a bargain.)[3]

Chuck and Patchen did something few teachers in our lives had done up until that point: believed in us, without bullshitting us about what was coming next in our lives. We were all fairly thirsty for the practicality they offered. Beyond the classes on how to balance a budget and the tangible reality of volunteer service, the backpacking trips were spaces for us to connect with something older, wilder, and bigger than our egos, and learn we were quite capable of self-reliance and figuring things out on our own (even if they were watching from the sidelines to ensure we didn't get killed). You don't have to be outwardly "troubled" to need this kind of experience. In fact, I think most teenagers need it quite badly.

The other misconception I hear after telling people about Team is that it must have been bewilderingly expensive—like some Montessori version of Boy Scouts, or something that exists only in New Zealand. But it wasn't. It was free and part of the public school district. To get in, you simply had to pass a two-question interview.[4]

Every few years, the school board threatens to shut the program down, under the not-entirely-faulty logic of "it's not fair to give this much attention to twenty-four kids and leave the other thousand kids in the school district out." Notwithstanding that Team raised a lot of its own money via car washes and bake sales, I'd like to counter that just because we can't make a difference for a thousand kids, doesn't mean we shouldn't make a difference for twenty-four. In fact, go ahead and make a difference for the

---

3. They did not.

4. Chuck and Patchen asked why you wanted to be there and what you hoped to get out of it. I spent a few sleepless nights trying to untangle the riddle of these deceptively simple questions. In retrospect, I think they were just checking whether we were the kind of person that was going to drop seven hits of acid the minute we were alone in the desert, wander off, die, and get the whole program shut down forever—not bad screening questions for life in general, if you think about it.

whole thousand, or more. Make Team a national option, please. The program is a miracle. I hope it lasts forever and ever, until the sun burns out.

Team was also where I met a girl named Jeanne, the friend who would become my backpacking buddy. At sixteen, Jeanne was a stoned, rainbow-goth Care Bear trapped in the body of a Swiss-Miss babysitter. She spent most of high school skinny-dipping, practicing yoga headstands, and talking about how much she wanted to go to India "because, like, pink is basically their black." She smoked unfathomable amounts of weed—but didn't care that I never took a puff. She carried around a never-ending supply of Pop-Tarts that she generously shared with me and is the only person I've ever met who unironically likes Cheez Whiz. Despite our outward differences in high school—I was a straight-edge, straitlaced, body-shy, insufferably emo kid—we had one very important thing in common: our desire to go outside, a lot.

We both agreed, although I can't remember ever talking about it, that there was some kind of magic in nature, a magic that would make everything better whenever we needed it to. We wanted to be drunk on it, overwhelmed by it. In the absence of any female role models for running out into the woods to connect with something spiritual (I think Cheryl Strayed was still on heroin at the time)—we became our own role models.

After we graduated from Team, caught somewhere between witchy-teen-girl urges and the heady high of having access to a car for the first time, we made it our mission to go on as many backpacking trips as our babysitting and catering job budgets would allow. We climbed boulders in Joshua Tree, slept in parking lots on NorCal's foggy Lost Coast, fell into quicksand in the slot canyons of Arizona, climbed the Zugspitze in Germany, and got lost on a volcano in Chile.

In all these adventures, it was Jeanne who had the car, the plan, the map, the Pop-Tarts, and the confidence. She is the Ilana Wexler to my Abbi Abrams; our trips often involved me telling her not to get in that guy's car or take drugs from strangers, and being genuinely surprised when she patiently explained that our creepy French couch-surfing host had actually been trying to have a threesome with us last week. She is the reason I ran off a cliff in Interlaken with a parachute on my back and almost fell into a molten sulfur pit in South America. If it wasn't for her, I may have never done anything interesting in my life at all.

Jeanne's attitude certainly spurred me on, but the truth is, she had most of the gear. I don't remember how she got it. Even though we grew up in a wealthy area, we were ragamuffins by comparison and couldn't afford to buy anything new. But whenever we needed a tent, extra stuff sack, or stove, Jeanne seemed to find a way to make one appear. When she moved to Germany in 2010, not only was I heartbroken to lose the only woman who understood my deep urge to run into nature as often as possible but I also lost my dealer. I had to figure out backpacking on my own now.

NOT EVERYONE IS LUCKY ENOUGH to have a free school program to teach them the basics of backpacking. However, I want to dispel the idea that there is no baby-step, self-taught process to get into backpacking—that you have to wait for a guru to arrive, or experience some kind of unforeseen life crisis that both invites and requires the liminal space of a multi-month, cross-country sojourn on the Pacific Crest or Appalachian Trails.

My guess is you probably want to backpack for one of two reasons: to test yourself or to run away from something. The good news is the testing comes pretty naturally. The bad news is running away isn't going to work.

At first, backpacking can feel like running away from your normal life, into something greater, more honest, more eternal. But at some point, you realize you only have yourself and whatever you brought with you, including your thoughts. In fact, in the backcountry, there is nowhere to run; you must instead face everything you've been running from. This doesn't necessarily need to take five months—a weekend trip can be just as effective, depending on the scope of your emotional problems and your desire to get things over with.

My longest backcountry trip to date was a hair under two weeks. To be clear, this isn't because I don't want to be out there longer—it's because I have never been able to drop out of my life for five months and then turn up like, "Hey guys. What's good? What's a 'Notice to Evict'?" And I don't even have a mortgage, any chronic illnesses, or kids.

I admire people who have done the famous multimonth through-hikes of the world, truly. But beyond "How did you handle the solitude?" "How did you organize your resupplies?" and "Tell me again how much your tent weighed?" I always want to ask, "How did you get all that time off?"

I don't think putting your entire life on hold for half a year should be a prerequisite for finding solace in the wilderness. In my humble opinion, quitting your job, shaving your head, and abandoning your responsibilities is the worst way to fantasize about backpacking. You do not need to be in crisis to deserve liminal space.

This book deals with a world where you *do* have unshakable obligations, permanent commitments, and helpless dependents—and still (or perhaps precisely because of those things), you want to give in to that screaming demand inside of you to abandon everything—just for a hot second—and submit yourself to the impassive all-mother of Nature.

To be clear, you can still hop right into something like the PCT with almost no training (let it be known that Cheryl Strayed is a boss bitch). A lot of people do, and most of them do not die out there. But, if you're interested in experiencing standard-issue backpacker's masochism without an added side of novice tears, let's talk about how to start where you are now, so that you can gracefully transform into an Olympian god who will eventually conquer mountains and make your exes immolate with envy when they see your Instagram feed.

EMBRACING YOUR BODY BECAUSE YOU DON'T HAVE A CHOICE ANYMORE

Most sports require equipment—balls and nets, paddles or little sticks to swing. In backpacking, the primary equipment is the giant blob on your back, and the mode of play is your body carrying it. Yes, you modify your body with things like shoes and clothing, but the entire sport is basically putting one foot in front of the other and remembering to breathe. Look down at your legs right now. That's it, buddy. That's what we're working with.

This is not to imply that you have to be in perfect physical condition to backpack. I've met seventy-year-olds who have crushed twenty-five miles a day on the Pacific Crest Trail, and people whose BMI is over 30 that have

"EVERYONE HERE IS WHITE"

At some point, numerous comedians thought it would be funny to classify camping and backpacking as a "white man's sport," because only white people could ever possibly call sleeping outside fun. Unfortunately, backpacking imagery has a history of confirming this perception, by featuring one notably colonial color. The good news is the reality on the ground is much more polychromatic.

If you're looking for outdoor friends that come in shades other than taupe and eggshell, check out Outdoor Afro, Wild Diversity, Brown People Camping, Latino Outdoors, Unlikely Hikers, and Diversify Outdoors for local groups and outings. Their members would love to connect, encourage, and share nature with you.

passed my ass goodbye going uphill. Being heavy or carrying an AARP card is not a dealbreaker. Knowing yourself and what your body can do is key.

Now granted, I am a white, thirty-something, non-disabled woman in possession of, according to an X-ray tech near the end of a twelve-hour shift, "some big ass lungs." I tick a lot of privilege boxes. But the one thing I'm not, and have never been, is skinny. I'm five foot ten, with a dress size of roughly 12 or 14, depending on how close it is to cake season.[5] Like any good and proper American teenage girl raised in the early 2000s, I spent most of my youth hating my body. I went on various diets because I didn't want to ruin "the best years of my life" being chubby (instead I ruined them by having low blood sugar and hating myself). Now I have reached a place where I eat my greens, do my cardio routines, and then just forgive whatever I see in the mirror, knowing I'm doing the best I can without crossing into obsession and insanity. However, I'd be kidding myself if I said I didn't envy the fleet-footedness of the small, thin backpackers who bound across trails like gazelles. They are faster than me and seem to have an easier time of everything, from adjusting to higher elevations to fitting into sleeping bags.

If, like me, you're built like a tree trunk, your legs and feet will do more work than if you're built like a stick rule. This is a fact that needs to be

---

5. This is whenever I want cake.

respected. But most people's muscles are proportional to their weight and height. What I lack in svelteness, I make up for in stamina. More importantly, backpacking is not a race. There are no points to win or trophies to hang. It is you and the earth. No one gives you permission to belong. You simply do.

Regardless of your build, there are some things you can do to make tackling this physical challenge easier. It doesn't matter whether you're thin or fat, short or tall—respecting your body's capabilities and limits is what matters. But first you must learn what they are.

TESTING YOUR LIMITS

The best way to begin backpacking is to start small. It's better to test your gear, learn what scares you, increase your level of difficulty, and get to know your body while you can still return home at night, reflect, and discover what makes you comfortable.

Step One: Day Hiking

Some people can hike twenty-five miles in a day. Others can hike four. Learning what you're capable of is the first step to planning a bigger trip, because it will determine the duration and difficulty of your days. Even if you're a proficient athlete, walking all day is different from other sports. Is a chronic injury going to flare up? Are your boots going to suddenly betray you? Do you even *like* being outside all day? We have no idea! Go exploring.

When you day hike, it's a good idea to wear the shoes, socks, and—if we're being honest—the backpack you'll be wearing on a multiday adventure. This helps acclimate your body to the actual challenges it will face out there. You'll look less weird if you try this in a regional park with hiking trails, but it also works on city sidewalks. However, if you're worried your neighbors will be alarmed by the sight of you walking your dog with a tundra-sized dump-sack gripping your hips and shoulders, another option is to put some weight in a regular day pack and carry it. Canned food, sacks of flour, or jugs of water work great, but in a pinch, your lucky bricks will do just fine.

You'll quickly discover how different hiking with a heavy load is. That's why backpackers are clinically obsessed with the weight of everything they carry. If you run into other hikers on a backcountry trail, it is customary to inquire about and compliment them on the feathery constitution of a piece of gear. The backpacker will then share its precise weight down to the ounce, possibly pulling up a spreadsheet on their phone, whereupon you may express admiration and wonder. After this ritual greeting, descriptions of upcoming water sources are exchanged, along with, perhaps, Jell-O pudding powders. If you practice hiking with bricks, remove them from your pack before you encounter other hikers to avoid any humiliation during this exchange.

On your day hikes, you'll naturally observe your body—especially if it starts complaining—but be sure to observe your mind as well. If you're like me and can't handle being alone with your thoughts for more than twenty minutes before openly weeping, bring a friend. This way you can banter and sing and share old memories to distract yourself from the heat-death of the universe. However, if you hate all your friends and decide to hike alone, pay attention to where your mind wanders. It's not easy to be alone with your own thoughts, without any kind of distraction, for days on end. Good for you if you can do it, but most people in the twenty-first century are functionally allergic to silence, even if they aren't aware of it. If you plan to backpack alone, it's a good idea to practice day hiking alone. It's an entirely different challenge from hiking with friends.

A lot of through-hikers who brave the trail alone use headphones to add a soundtrack to their adventure or take comfort in the familiar voices of podcast hosts. There's no shame in pulling out some digital company. I have been on twelve-mile day hikes where, around mile eight, I just can't take it anymore and pull out my headphones. (This is how I have come to associate the tweaker grinding of Skrillex with the gentle scent of a sun-baked forest floor.) Sometimes, however, with my headphones in, I worry that I'm missing the healing harmonies of birdsong or perhaps the soft padding of a serial killer sneaking up on me. This is why, even though I bring headphones on a day hike, I never hike with my headphones in when I'm backpacking, especially if there aren't any other people around.

Step Two: Base Camping

Once you've gotten a little taste of the great outdoors, and then returned safely home to your shower and bed, let's up the ante by removing those

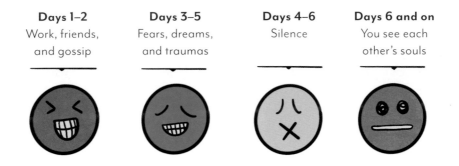

Days 1–2	Days 3–5	Days 4–6	Days 6 and on
Work, friends, and gossip	Fears, dreams, and traumas	Silence	You see each other's souls

Evolution of a conversation during a backpacking trip

last two comforts. There are two ways to go about this: one is car camping; the other is base camping, a.k.a. walk-in camping.

Car camping is basically bringing your car to a generously sized, tree-lined parking lot in the middle of nowhere and then sleeping next to it. It usually smells like nice forest things and maybe some barbeque, but it also sounds like a playground. I car camped a lot with my friends in high school. One of us would borrow their mom's minivan, and we would pool all our money to get twenty packages of mac 'n cheese, fifty packs of gummy bears, Cheetos, Pop-Tarts, spaghetti, Top Ramen, two wheels of Brie, and three cans of soup each (to be safe), before driving somewhere we had read about online while fighting over who had ten dollars in cash for the campsite fee. We would park the car, set up the private mini-mart we had purchased, and unfurl the twenty-year-old tent my mom had used when we were kids. The weekend was spent more or less horizontally, with one of us occasionally getting up to move burning logs from one firepit to another, or make a tin-foil oven to cook the fish our friend Danielle had caught.[6]

At some point I would try to find a hiking trail, which is how I quickly learned that not all campgrounds have hiking trails. You'd think they would, but they don't. Sometimes campgrounds are just beautiful parking lots. At "top-rated" Kirk Creek Campground overlooking the central California coast, you can hear traffic from your tent.

---

6. By "caught," I mean she left camp in a bikini and came back twenty minutes later with a confused guy holding out six fish.

I like car camping a lot. (I still do it at least twice a year.) But car camping doesn't really prepare you for backpacking because it's usually an exercise in ironic decadence rather than minimalism. You can test how warm your sleeping bag and clothing will be, maybe even how your stove will perform—and that's about it.

Base camping gets you a little closer to the real deal. This is when you hike in, anywhere from half a mile to half a day, to a backcountry site with minimal to no amenities or infrastructure. You set up a home base, and then each morning shoot off like a bee on a different trail, returning to your little nest at night. It's quite lovely, and the lack of flush toilets, beer-peddling concessionaires, and plug-ins for amps tends to deter the more casual crowd. It's a great way to dip your toe in the backpacking water, so to speak. You're overcoming the psychological barrier of sleeping outside, far away from the safety of your car, but without the physical annoyance of packing up everything and carrying it out every single morning.

Step Three: Multinight Backpacking

One of the ironies in backpacking is that how you pack for a three-day trip is almost exactly the same as how you pack for a multimonth trip, with the notable exception of how much food you'll carry.[7] You'll need the same shoes, water filter, clothes, stove, headlamp, and poo shovel whether you're going out for a weekend, or a week, or a month.

Furthermore, the first day of your backpacking trip (really, the first night) is always the hardest. Always. Your pack is probably the heaviest it will be, you won't sleep very well, but above all, you're insecure as hell. With each step you take away from the parking lot, doubts will swarm above you like locusts, infecting your every thought. "Was this a good idea?" "What if I get hurt?" "What if I get lonely?" "How do I go this long without Wi-Fi?" Every single time I go out, at the end of that first day—after watching the heavens tear themselves apart in a watercolor of peaches and ambers and periwinkle blues, the sun kiss the lip of the horizon goodbye, the last

---

7. Even on monster trails like the Pacific Crest, Continental Divide, and Appalachian Trails, people must necessarily duck out off the trail every week or so for food resupplies. (And maybe a hot shower and a bed while they're in town, why not?)

The tamer versus the tamee

indigos of twilight exhale, and night settle like a blanket on the earth—I calmly put away all my things, crawl into my sleeping bag, look at the ceiling of my tent, and think, "This is it. I am going to die."

This is why, if you're going to go to the trouble of planning a backpacking trip, it is best to go out for as long as you possibly can. Not because you'll necessarily do a better job of finding yourself, but because waking up after that first night and realizing you're alive, and still have ten fingers and ten toes, is the greatest rush of self-confidence I've ever experienced outside of a bass drop at midnight at an EDM festival. Once you pass that hurdle, the rest of the trip becomes truly enjoyable. By day four or five, you are addicted to the open sky, self-sufficiency, and lack of a beeping, tweeting device constantly jamming your mental feed. Deep in some kind of masochistic feedback loop, you don't want to go home. You're *in it*.

SELECTING YOUR BACKPACKING BUDDY

Most people who enter nature fall into one of two categories: those who seek to tame it and those who seek to be tamed by it. The "tamers" are usually ex–Boy Scouts, buried somewhere under sixty pounds of gear, usually the more expensive versions of what you are carrying. They got their permits six months ago, have memorized seven books on how to disable a bear mid-attack, and have an up-to-date CPR certificate. They're not having a good time unless they feel like they are "being tested," and/or you are behind them. They have a Garmin. And a Fitbit. And a GoPro.

The "tamees" are too full of gratitude for nature's bounty to bother with the nuances of gear planning. This is why they are constantly borrowing your bug spray and sunscreen. They might pass you, but it's not to make you feel bad, it's only because they are so in the moment that they didn't notice you. They say "thank you" a lot. They will be the first person to help you if you get hurt. They also need your hair tie.

Most people recommend you pair up with others of your same type. I disagree. The Boy Scouts need the gratitude fairies to teach them that you get more joy from being in the moment than you do from stress and pressure and competition. Similarly, the fairies need the Boy Scouts for stove fuel and lip balm.

Speed is the real deciding factor. It's best to walk with someone who isn't going to be annoying and stir crazy if you only want to hike five or six miles a day, or drag you down if you're on a schedule that requires fifteen-plus-mile days.

Pace aside, there's personality to consider. You may discover that someone you thought you wanted to spend five solid days with is actually someone you don't want to be around for more than ten minutes. Similarly, someone you think you have nothing in common with may transform into a new family member after a single sweaty, tear-stained week.

Day hiking is a great way to determine whether you want to backpack with someone. If you don't already have a buddy in mind, it's a good idea to find one (day hikes with large groups organized by outdoor retail stores and online communities work well for this), not just because they can keep you from becoming lonely, but also so there's someone to run for help if anything goes horribly, horribly wrong. (But it won't. Don't think about that. Everything will be totally fine.)

Chapter 2

GEAR
Let's Spend $2,000 in the Name of Minimalism

"All you need is two axes, good rope, and a tin cup."
    —Someone trying to sell a book

Backpacking is a meditation, a ritual, an entire religion centered on the idea of minimalism. I'm not speaking explicitly about ultralight backpacking, a label you'll see in gear descriptions and thrown around on backpacking forums that often just means, "I'm rich and can afford silk." In general backpacking gear is ideally as light as possible—in terms of the number of items you carry, their volume, and their weight. The private fantasy of most backpackers is to take the last swig from their water bottle, feel a breeze, and realize they've floated away into the sky. If Osprey could make a helium tank that doubled as a travel pillow, every guy in Silicon Valley would have two. At REI they actually have a scale, like in ancient Egyptian wall carvings, where Anubis weighs your pack against a feather; if it's heavier, you get cursed to wander all-hours-generator-powered RV parks for the rest of your life (if it's lighter, you get to skip the line to summit Everest).

The obsession is logical, though. You are going to be carrying *every single item* you need on your back. Individual ounces seem insignificant until hundreds of them add up—before you know it, you've got eighty pounds resting on your shoulders for a simple weekend trip. I don't know what else you read before you got here, but just to be clear: there's no reason to take a hunting axe backpacking, and you should under no circumstances bring a cast-iron pan. Backpacking is the opposite vibe from the "pioneer" branch of returning to nature. Rather, it is the art of moving through the wilderness as if you were a ghost, a mood that is actually codified into one of the few holy rules of backpacking.

LEAVING NO TRACE

"Leave No Trace" is the aggressive instruction (if not outright plea) given by every park and forestry service that oversees wildlands the world over. It means that you should pass through nature as though you were completely invisible. Sometimes you'll see this concept phrased as "take only photos, leave only footprints" or "pack it in, pack it out," but these are just different ways of saying that wherever you walk, camp, sing, cook, or cry for mercy to any god who will listen, you should make sure no one else will ever know it ever happened except you.

But what does LNT actually look like in the field? Sure, there's the obvious stuff like picking up your plastic cheese stick wrappers and not dumping your soapy dishwater into that sparkling lake. But LNT also means uncomfortable, annoying stuff, like setting up your camp at least two hundred feet from a lake or river, packing out your used toilet paper, and burying your poop in a hole at least six inches deep. Sometimes, it means bizarre stuff, like wandering to the intertidal zone at the ocean, and taking a dump right there in front of god and country (lakes are princesses but the ocean forgives everything, apparently).

You might be thinking this kind of behavior is insane—you're kind of right. The whole point of wilderness is that it's supposed to be vast and untamed, oblivious to me and my puny mortal shuffles, right? It is in civilization that I must be conscientious and neighborly and aware of the space I take up; what's the point of coming out here if I can't be in the moment and think only of myself?

It's true—when you backpack, you're signing up to take a break from your usual routine (apparently by having a fun and novel time burying your own feces). But when it comes to thinking about how you affect space, unfortunately, no, thinking about your impact is still on the to-do list. Not only do you have to think about wild animals that, for everyone's benefit, you want to keep wild (and away from you and your stuff at one in the morning) but you also have to think about other people, the people who will come to this place after you're gone, chasing that same "Lewis and Clark discovering America" fantasy you're chasing now. Because that's exactly what it is: a fantasy.

It breaks my heart to say this, but in the twenty-first century, nothing on earth is truly pristine. The era of Lewis and Clark and Sacagawea was a long time ago, and the feeling of primordial ecstasy you get while walking through a deep, untamed wilderness is in fact the intentional, hard-won product of a succession of lawmakers, nonprofits, friends-of organizations, and other backpackers who have been collectively working their asses off to ensure that when you, noob, finally get there, you get to pretend no one else has ever been there before. The minute you set foot in the wilderness, you are the beneficiary—and also the newest member—of this vanguard of protection.

Leave No Trace runs on the honor system by necessity. Amazingly, most people observe these practices, but not everyone. You'll know the failures when you see them: dirty campsites covered in beer cans, toilet paper blossoms tangled in shrubs, and names carved into trees. These kinds of messes tempt rangers into closing trails and forbidding access to some sections of wilderness entirely. Don't add to this temptation.

If you've read a lot of Sartre, hate the world, and don't really care about your fellow man or whether or not he interacts with your trash, then at least consider the animals. A lot of bears out there would gladly come into your camp and kill you for that lemon-cookie-flavored energy bar wrapper you left on the ground (or in your tent).

PACKING LIGHT

Now that we've covered what you can't leave in the wilderness, let's move on to what you should take with you in the first place. You may find yourself overwhelmed by options while shopping for equipment: "Do I want a tactical nylon stretch hammock pant? Or a cargo space knife towel shirt? What's the difference between Merino wool and . . . wool? What is DriDown?" Every item's description will make it sound like it's the greatest thing since sliced bread and will seem to insist that you need—*need*—it to be happy and clean and safe outside.

The first time I prepped for a trip on my very own, without the guidance of my mom or my teachers or Jeanne, I bought everything I thought I needed in a hurry, and for cheap, online. I barely thought about what any of it weighed, assuming, since I was only going out for a weekend, that my food would account for most of my pack weight. I didn't really have to worry about the weight of things like my clothes, my stove, or my sleeping bag, right? So I stuffed everything I thought I might need (or want) into my large, 75-liter backpack the night before my trip, hoisted it onto my back, and looked in the mirror.

I was teetering at a ninety-degree angle underneath an orange shell on my back the size of Denver. I looked like the world's unhappiest Teenage Mutant Ninja Turtle. I was supposed to walk uphill in this? The pack squeaked. The turtle face in the mirror fell into a concerning frown.

My point is the weight adds up faster than you think it will, especially when you're on a budget, because the weight of a piece of backpacking gear is usually inversely proportional to its price. It's not impossible to have a light pack on a budget—you're just going to have to exercise some serious prudence about what you buy. It also means that you have permission to look at something and say "no, actually, that's not for me." (If you're a person who has a lot of trouble saying no to things out of an overabundance of caution and fear of being caught unprepared, this is going to feel really hard. And that's OK too.)

The number one thing you should look for when shopping for gear—regardless of an item's advertised use or where it's being sold—is its weight, usually in the item's description or on its tag. If it isn't easy to find, that's your first clue that something is amiss. All backpackers are *obsessed* with the weight of their gear. So if a company didn't think to include weight under "more details," that's a huge indicator that they weren't designing their product for backpackers at all.

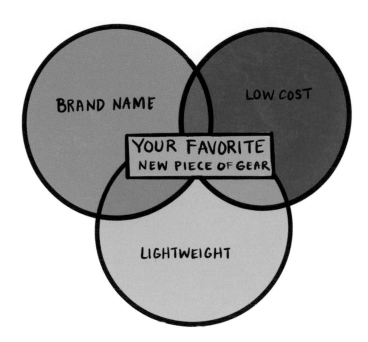

The holy trinity of backpacking gear

Once you see the weight, ask yourself if there's a similar item that is equally priced, made by an equally reputable brand, that weighs less. The holy trinity of a high-quality backpacking item is low cost, brand name, and lightweight.

You need not—dare I say, should not—buy most of your backpacking gear new. The only things I'd actually recommend you buy new are your socks (and even then you could wash them, but like, ew, used socks). You can get an astounding amount of gear secondhand, or on deep clearance, and what you can't purchase new or used, you can probably borrow, either (rented) from a store or (free!) from a friend.

Borrowing Gear

There are likely a few people in your life who once bought everything they needed for a backpacking trip, and, upon returning home immediately pitched it into the basement, swearing they would never, ever do that again (this definitely will not happen to you). These sad tents and forlorn stoves sit there now, drooping, forgotten, ticking away the time left on their warranties.

Go save them. Post about what you are looking for on Facebook, or Instagram, or whatever social media platform you flick through when you're supposed to be at work, and behold the results: an amazing amount of gear will present itself to be borrowed for free.

How do I know this is going to work? Because backpacking has a tendency to bring out everyone's altruistic side, as if harkening back to a primordial time when man's common enemy was nature, not each other, and we all needed to stick together for survival. I would trip your grandmother to get the last seat on a light rail car in San Francisco, but I've literally taken off the pants I was wearing and given them to someone in need on the trail. Along the spine of all the famous multimonth routes in America (the Appalachian Trail, the Pacific Crest Trail, the Continental Divide Trail), you will stumble upon gigantic chests full of food, shoes, fuel, and all manner of useful bric-a-brac left out by backpackers, for other backpackers to take, just in case they need it. It's fucking beautiful.

The catch to the volley of free backpacks and stoves and headlamps that will likely apparate once you ask for them is that you have to give them back in better condition than when you borrowed them. However, unless you literally throw a backpack into a ditch, trample on it, and invite some elk to poop in it, that shouldn't be hard to do: most backpacking gear is built to withstand the elements, and ostensibly handle some serious abuse. That's kind of the whole point.[8]

Renting Gear

I accidentally bought a bunch of gear before I found out about rental programs, but perhaps it was for the best. With my luck, I'd pay fifty dollars to rent a tent, hear a hedgehog fighting a dinosaur outside in the middle of the night, and slice a hole in the side panel to escape before realizing I was

---

8. See: Me, age seventeen, trying to borrow an ultralight cookpot from my mother, and her saying with a wagging finger and a warning tone, "This is titanium. It's very expensive. Do not do anything to it, or you owe me a new one." To which I replied, "If you paid one hundred dollars for a titanium pot, and I managed to do anything to it, am I really the one who has swindled you?"

half asleep. The next day I'd sullenly return it to the store, where the dude behind the counter would ring me up $450 for a tent five other people got trench foot in.

Maybe I have mistakenly assumed that all gear rental counters operate like car leasing agencies, where there's always a catch that means I'll end up paying more than if I had bought something used. I'm probably wrong, so I'm not saying you shouldn't rent gear—especially if you're trying backpacking out for the first time. Or, maybe you already have gear, but you just need a slightly different tent or bag for one trip.

Renting can be a serious godsend—for instance, if you're planning on a one-way trip, you can sometimes pick up a bear canister at the ranger station near your starting trailhead, and then return it to another station when you exit, fifty miles away. But be sure to read the fine print about what happens to your deposit if you don't bring that stuff back. Backpackers are good people. Companies who rent things to backpackers aren't necessarily good too.

Though rarely advertised, many REIs across the US rent gear for several different outdoor activities, including backpacking. Depending on what

A FIELD GUIDE TO BACKPACKING STORES

» **REI:** First of Its Name, the Unimpressed, Queen of the Experts and the First Timers, Protector of Idiots, and Mother of Backpackers

» **Cabela's:** REI's Republican cousin

» **Amazon:** Your clearinghouse for cheap Chinese knockoffs

» **Big 5:** For when you want to play lacrosse on Everest

» **Sports Basement:** Stealthily running America's largest backpacking gear rental program from stores throughout California since 1998

» **Your local mom-and-pop store:** That helpful one that you forgot existed

» **Goodwill:** A slot machine of American knickknacks that sometimes spits out Patagonia down vests and Kelty tents

» **Sierra:** The Sprouts to REI's Whole Foods

» **Military surplus stores:** Amazing, so long as you don't mind looking like an extra on *Duck Dynasty* city you are in, you might be able to find local shops that rent gear, as well. The local shops charge about the same as the big guys, and have similarly high-quality gear, so use whatever recent propaganda you've read about supporting small businesses or the power of corporations to clean oceans and change the world to decide where you'd like to spend your money.

Buying Used Gear

Remember those people who went backpacking once and then swore they would never ever repeat the experience? (Again, this will absolutely not happen to you.) Good news: you can buy their shit for pennies on the dollar on eBay. I don't ask how a pair of brand-new Timberland boots with tags ends up on there for $39.99. I'm just happy to buy them. It's also the only place I've been able to find crystal iodine (for water purification) since it got banned because people use it to cook meth. Again . . . just . . . buy what you need, and don't ask too many questions.

For a less morally dubious shopping experience, in big cities especially, there are a lot of mom-and-pop outdoor stores that sell or even specialize in used gear (for example, Ascent Outdoors in Seattle or Young's Backpacking in Berkeley). Being able to touch and try on gear before you buy it usually saves you a lot of time and money compared to shopping online. Because backpacking is a physical hobby, it's nice to touch things before you buy them. If you have the option in your area, go in person.

In the event that, by the time you're reading this, we've reached the part of our digitally dystopian future where all the mom-and-pops have closed in your area, you have one more option. Most REIs have a hidden section in the back, past the kayaks and the clearance racks, where used-once-and-then-changed-my-mind gear is for sale. You can pick it up, play with it, and test it out; someone might even come over and help you.

Buying Clearance Gear

The difference between buying used and buying clearance is really more about your politics than your checkbook, as the two are often the same price. Do you want to keep something out of a landfill, or do you just want to save your money? Even if it's the latter, be wary. There are dozens of "super discount backpacking" stores online nowadays, and reviewing all of them here would amount to nothing more than a ridiculous commercial. However, as long as you don't mind wearing last season's shade of khaki or whether your sleeping bag is filled with ultralightdown as opposed to downultralight, you can make a real killing in the clearance section of most outdoor retail stores.

Then there's Amazon. Of course there is tons of gear on Amazon. But you're more likely to get hoodwinked there than helped. I know this from experience. While I've gotten fantastic, completely affordable rain pants and a brand-name stove on Amazon, that's as far as my luck has gone. Amazon plays host to a lot of cheap knockoff items that will try—sometimes very convincingly—to masquerade as high quality.

But the real trouble, honestly, is that Amazon reviews are deceptive. I'm not even talking about fake reviews. I'm taking about reviews titled "THIS WATER BOTTLE CHANGED MY LIFE" by someone who has never taken the object in question beyond the turbid wilds of their own backyard. I recommend you avoid shopping for gear there as much as possible.

Buying Brand-New Gear

You can go to a few different stores for new gear (see the list at the beginning of this chapter), but there's one that you'll probably find yourself lost in more than once while prepping for your first trip. Every time I have been in an REI, I feel like I'm in a yacht club for practicing druids; I'm not sure I belong, but it all smells so nice and they have everything I've ever wanted to take outside. I also consistently do double takes at the price tags: the truth is, almost anything you see can be purchased cheaper elsewhere. However, the real draw of REI is its ability to completely understand you and accept you for who you are—for a fee. It's like going to your therapist's office, but with kayaks and freeze-dried cheese rations.

Every single person I've ever interacted with at REI has answered my questions without a hint of patronization, even when it's abundantly clear that I am a danger to myself and others. They once gave me a full refund on a pair of sunglasses that I broke on the first day of a backpacking trip, lost most pieces of, and didn't have the receipt for. I walked up to the counter holding nothing but one shiny plastic temple and half a hinge, with a fully rehearsed polite-but-firm sermon of injustice. I barely got through my opening sentence—"these broke on my first use"—before the unreasonably aerobicized sales clerk just started shoving dollars into my hands. It is Elysium. Bring money.

CHOOSING YOUR BACKPACK

When you begin amassing your gear, the first thing you'll want to acquire is your new partner in crime, the one who's going to be with you through it all: your backpack. If you were like me growing up, you had a backpack you took to school, with helpful stuff thrown into it haphazardly. Sometimes you'd rummage through it and find a Lisa Frank pen (awesome) or last week's sandwich (less awesome). Most of its weight would sit squarely on your shoulders, giving you constant backaches despite the fact that it weighed only twenty to thirty pounds. After a year or two, it probably fell apart.

Those days are behind you. If the humble schoolchild's backpack is the luggage equivalent of a college dorm room, a backpacking backpack is a twenty-room mansion with secret tunnels and a dumbwaiter. It can condense, expand, tighten, transfer weight, separate, and then rejoin like Voltron. It is the peak of man's achievement in luggage.

These backpacks have a lot of special features (see the anatomy of a backpack illustration on the facing page), each designed to guide you on how to pack it. At the top is the brain, a little pouch that sits behind its namesake. Use it for maps, medicine, your pack cover, snacks, and other small items you want easy access to on the trail. The brain undercarriage is typically reserved for butt stuff (toilet paper, hand sanitizer, used wipes, etc.). The roomy interior of the pack is best for food and clothing (some people like to stow a warm jacket at the top).

The side pouches are great for storing things like your stove and water filter, and some packs also have a second pair of side pockets right behind your hips that fit water bottles. The hidey-hole at the bottom, sometimes with its own zipper, is designed for your sleeping bag. The hip belt, magically attaching this mass to your midsection, usually has pockets, one on each side. Use these to store snacks, lip balm, or anything else you don't want falling out of the pockets of your pants.

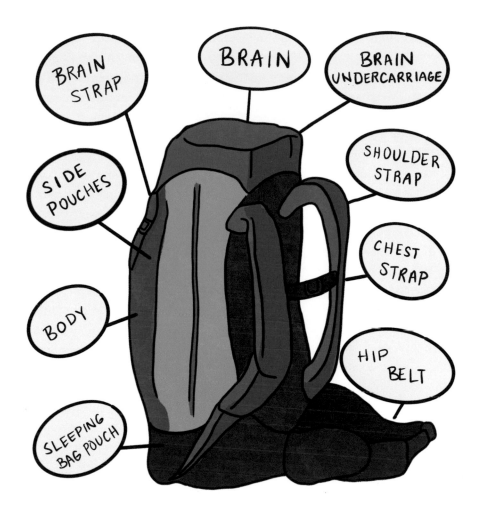

Generally speaking, backpacking packs come in three volume classifications: weekend trips (40 liters), three-to-five-day trips (60 liters), and
extended journey (75+ liters). My backpack is a 75-liter Dana Design from
the mid-90s. It's heavy and canvas, it's an ultralight backpacker's nightmare, and if you want it, you'll have to pry it out of my cold, dead hands. It's
a hazard-orange masterpiece that I bought used after a life-altering experience borrowing someone else's Dana pack in 2015.

Dana Design is a backpacking brand with a cult following; "Is that a
Dana?" is a phrase that followed me around various campgrounds and

backpacker shuttles in South America in 2016. Legend holds that its bags were once hand-stitched in the wilds of Montana by a mysterious shaman named Dana, but then the company totally sold out in the early 2000s to a cartel of Mexican sweatshops and is, like, super bad now. (The truth is Dana Gleason and Renee Sippel-Baker sold their heroically expanding company to K2 in 1995, who then became Marmot, who then killed the name "Dana," but kept the technology, which is still present today in Marmot's packs on countless store shelves. Meanwhile, Dana and Renee went on to found Mystery Ranch, where they appear to be taking hundreds of thousands of dollars from the military doing what they love best: obsessing over the perfect pack design. Good for them.)

I discovered the old-school Danas after borrowing my sister's roommate's Terraplane model, stuffing it with sixty pounds of crap, and taking it into the Patagonia backcountry for eight days. There, a miracle happened: I never got sore. Pause. Do you understand what I'm saying to you? I hiked over one hundred miles with sixty pounds on my back, and I wasn't sore or stiff anywhere. That's not supposed to happen. Normally, you wake up each morning of backpacking with chapped hips, swollen collarbones, and shoulders that feel like they went through a meat grinder. Waking up with no back pain in the backcountry, while perhaps normal for others, had certainly never happened to me before.

Ultralight hikers keep telling me my ancient Dana Design pack will forever bar me from the annals of featherweight glory, but I don't care what other people say about us. Packs are like lovers. When you find a good one— one that holds you, never hurts you, and supports your shoulders through trauma—never let it go.

To find your perfect pack, you can dizzy yourself with forum gossip about which brand is better than which, and the differences between 420-denier ripstop nylon and diamond ripstop polyurethane-coated polyamide. But the biggest factor, in my humble opinion, that actually determines what pack is right for you is its height.

Packs come in the same sizes as T-shirts—small, medium, and large— but your backpack size has nothing to do with your T-shirt size. Instead, it's determined by the length of your spine, from the bottom of your neck to the top of your hips. The good and proper thing to do is to go into an outdoor recreation store and, like a premium bra, get yourself fitted for a backpack. But if you're like me, and find the idea of strangers touching your body with measuring tape completely horrifying, you can also take your own measurements at home.

To measure the length of your spine, first, stand up tall, like god is watching. If you have a friend, call them forth. If you don't have a friend, stretch out your shoulder joints, and get ready to wriggle like a Muppet. Grab a soft measuring tape, and measure straight down from the base of your neck to the top of your pelvic bone (the area where your hips begin to widen). This might be a bit higher on your back than you think, so be sure to check in a mirror if you don't have a friend to place the bottom of the measuring tape in the right place. Note your spine length, and let the shopping begin.

Like bras, shoes, and skinny jeans that leave you crying in the fitting room stall, backpack sizes are inconsistent between brands. Generally speaking, however, a small is 16–18 inches long, a medium is 19–21 inches, and a large is 22–24 inches. Your final size might startle you, but remember, it has nothing to do with your clothing size. I am almost five eleven

HOW TO PUT ON YOUR BACKPACK

Unlike a school backpack, most of your backpacking backpack's weight will sit on your hips, like happy twin toddlers. This allows you to perform the miracle of hauling half your body weight up a mountainside without it really hurting very much. To put on a backpack, follow these steps:

1. Throw your pack onto your back like it's a cross you have to bear—kidding. The safest way to put on a backpack is to first loosen the straps. Then pick up the pack by the haul loop and hoist it onto your

right thigh, with your knee bent slightly. You can then slide your right shoulder into the shoulder strap and shift it onto your back.

2. To tighten the straps and adjust the fit, grab both ends of the hip belt, and click them into place just above your junk. The hip belt should rest directly over your hip bones.

3. Tighten the straps until your stomach looks like an overfilled muffin top.

4. Take your shoulder straps in both hands, and tighten them by pulling down like you're trying to kill the muffin top with triceps push-ups.

5. Attach the chest strap and tighten lightly—not so much you can't breathe, but enough to stabilize the top of your pack on your back.

6. Grab the straps behind your head and pull them down, like the legs of a toddler that you'll kick off your back if it doesn't stop flailing.

7. You should feel like your pack is teetering off your hips, with about an inch between your shoulder and the shoulder strap. Adjusted properly, it should feel like more of your weight is being carried by your hips, not your shoulders. Good job—you're on your way to becoming a chiropractor's dream.

and have been carrying around a respectably rotund pooch since puberty; size "medium" clothing has not fit me since I was in the fifth grade. And yet, a medium backpack fits perfectly. Even if fashion has no idea what to do with me, the backpacking world considers my spine completely unremarkable and sufficiently serviced by standard issue materials. I'll be honest—it's kind of nice. Anyway, most brands have a size chart in the store or online (this can be referenced even if you're purchasing used) as well. Be sure to double-check it before you buy, to make sure you're getting the correct size.

If you're between sizes, take into account the measurement of the hip belt and/or the suggested waist size to help determine if you should go up or down. Virtually every strap on a backpack can be adjusted by several inches, however, so don't stress massively about this. You can also seek out backpack manufacturers (such as Osprey, Gregory, and ULA) that allow you to swap out different size hipbelts with the main body if you

BASIC MULTIDAY BACKPACKING LIST

This is everything I take in my pack and how I order it:

THE BOTTOM OF THE PACK

1. Sleeping bag in its stuff sack
2. Sleeping pad (can also be attached to the exterior of your pack)

THE MIDDLE OF THE PACK

3. Food
4. Utensil, pot, and lid (plus a cup and serving dishes, if you're fancy)
5. Bear canister (if applicable)
6. Stove
7. Fuel
8. Shelter system (including tent body, poles, rain fly, and footprint)

THE TOP OF THE PACK

9. Two pairs of pants
10. Two shirts
11. Two pairs of underwear (sports bras, panties)
12. Two pairs of socks
13. Base layer
14. Mid-layer
15. Shell layer
16. A beanie or buff

THE BRAIN OF THE PACK

17. A medicine kit (tweezers, gauze, iodine, painkillers, anti-diarrheal medication, antihistamines, adhesive bandages, emergency blanket)
18. A toiletry kit (mini toothpaste, toothbrush, salve)
19. Headlamp and extra batteries
20. Map(s)
21. Firestarter
22. Pack cover
23. Water purification system
24. Sunscreen
25. Insect repellant (as needed)

26. Gaffer tape
27. Knife

THE UNDERSIDE OF THE BRAIN

28. Toilet paper (stored in a clean ziplock bag)
29. A bag to stash used toilet paper (contained within a larger ziplock for double protection and usually covered in duct tape)
30. Orange shovel
31. Hand sanitizer

THE OUTSIDE OF THE PACK

32. Two cotton bandanas, taking their sun bath (one for body washing, one for wiping)
33. Hiking poles
34. Other stabby items like ice axes and crampons (if headed for the snow)
35. Permits, if applicable
36. Personal locator beacon or satellite messenger
37. Any other items that couldn't fit in my pack (sleeping pad, camp shoes, or tent poles)

That should do you. Some people also like to carry a deck of playing cards or a small journal and a pen. This is usually a good idea. You may find yourself drawn to poetry and other acts of fancy, even if you're not normally like that at home. You're going on an adventure. Welcome the muse.

are someone who typically falls outside of whatever the hell the outdoor industry considers "normal" body measurement ranges.

I know this seems like a lot of work now, but you're saving yourself bottles of painkillers and hours begging campmates for massages later. Trust me, it's worth it.

If, by chance, you are not in a financial position to be buying a new, or even used backpack, and are pretty much at the mercy of whatever is in your friend's mom's cousin's sister's boyfriend's garage . . . that's OK, too. Again, almost everything on a backpack can be adjusted, including the height and width of the straps. You might have to spend more time fiddling with straps on a pack that's slightly big or small for you, and you may reach a point where no matter what you do, you have to accept you will never achieve a "perfect" fit. However, there's a pretty good chance you can attain a "good enough" fit. And good enough is just that. The search for perfect gear can quickly become a time-sucking, dragon-chasing enterprise. Just pack yourself some extra gummy worms. You'll be fine. Probably.

Anyway, once you find your new partner in crime, it should last through decades of sun, wind, and rain. Despite the fact that backpacking companies advertise their products as something that will last the rest of your life, they seem to come out with new models every year. This has never made sense to me, but the good news is that it tends to create an overstock. Sales are generally easy to find.

BEDAZZLING YOUR BACKPACK

Like a thirteen-year-old girl discovering Claire's for the first time, your pack enjoys accessorizing. Here are a few things you'll want to take along so your pack feels its best while out in the wild.

Pack Cover

Pack covers are fifty-dollar accessories that keep the contents of your pack dry in the face of rain, storms, or even overnight dew, and prevent the fabric from soaking up pounds of water. If you don't want to spend fifty dollars on a pack cover, you can also buy a gigantic plastic poncho to drape over your pack—and possibly even you—while you walk. I got my pack cover at Goodwill for fifty cents. Your call.

Stuff Sacks

Stuff sacks are especially tough bags that store gear, keeping the interior of your pack from resembling the closet of an angsty teen. How you organize your pack is a matter of personal preference, but the basic idea is to protect your food and clothes from rain and cross contamination with other objects (you don't really want your water filter getting any ideas from your dirty underwear). You can definitely use plastic trash bags to accomplish the same task, but if you don't want your backpack to perpetually look like your curb on garbage night, you can buy the pretty, candy-colored sacks they sell at virtually every outdoor gear store.

Compression Sacks

A compression sack is a special class of stuff sack with straps on the exterior, allowing you to put anything inside and mash it down as much as your strength (and the bag's constitution) will allow—kind of like a manual vacuum sealer. Compression sacks are key for squishing your sleeping bag down so that it fits into your pack, but they also come in handy for reducing the bulk of clothing, tent bodies, or any other soft thing you happen to bring along.

Because of how much compression stresses the seams, it's a good idea to buy compression sacks new and to stick with brand names. A cheap one will last a few trips before needing to be replaced. A good one will last you the rest of your life.

GOING STRAPLESS

When I was seventeen, my mother cut the straps off all the backpacks in the house. Borrowing one for a trip, I found a deflated nylon supersock that eerily resembled a backpack I once knew. My mother responded, "Straps are dead weight. Put everything inside your pack." My sleeping pad lived on the outside of my pack. "Where will I attach it now?" I asked. She told me to figure it out. And, with great nail biting and rationing, I eventually did.

To this day, you can find packs that claim to do it all in one streamlined, waterproof, expandable pouch. There's no reason not to look very seriously at a pack dubbed "ultralight" while shopping. But I wouldn't recommend cutting the straps off an older, used pack. It won't know what to do with itself. Even the most expensive ultralight packs have compartments, mesh pockets, and an outside strap or two.

NOW THAT WE'VE TALKED A bit about packs, let's talk about how to protect and cover the other critical, more fragile object we'll be bringing into the wilderness: you.

Chapter 3

CLOTHES
How to Not Get Killed by Your Jeans

"The worse it smells, the better it works."
—A backpacking expert

"You shouldn't wear those pants." I was talking to my friend in a tone that I hoped expressed caution, but not so much concern that I triggered some kind of testosterone-fueled teenage rebellion flashback. Most people don't like being told what to do in the woods—especially by seemingly incompetent pudgy girls. He had already graciously agreed to let me drag him away from the warm, loving purr of his custom gaming PC and out into the crisp air of the rocky, pine-filled lower Sierra Nevada in March.

I didn't want to push my luck, but we were also right at the snow line. These were bad conditions for jeans. In fact, it was a miracle my two-wheel drive hatchback had even made it up here without whirling backward like a Mario Kart hit by a green turtle shell.

"I only brought these pants," he countered.

I wanted to sigh. Loudly. I wanted to womansplain to him both that jeans are a terrible idea in this mushy weather, and that we talked about this before we left (because we definitely, definitely talked about this before we left).

But I didn't do either of these things. You sort of learn to pick your battles with some people. Plus, it was too late now (it wasn't like there was a Target anywhere out here), and we were only going out for the day anyway. We had spent the night before in a nearby campground, sneaking in at midnight, laughing at the exorbitant camping fee of thirty-five dollars, and setting up our tent in an apparently empty campsite. We were awakened by a woman rattling our tent like a bell at five in the morning, tersely informing us, "You're in our reservation." We hastily packed up our tent, apologized in that shitty way that people do when they're not actually sorry (just sorry you caught them), and with literally nowhere else to go, headed for the trailhead. It was now six o'clock, the temperature was forty-three degrees, and the sky was pregnant with rain clouds. Neither one of us had had coffee, and my hiking partner was wearing jeans.

"What's so bad about jeans?" he asked.

"They'll soak up all the water on the trail and they won't dry. You'll be walking in wet denim for six hours. They'll be heavy, and you'll be freezing."

His face changed, as if I was suddenly offering a dare. Like any minute he would start putting rocks in his backpack, just to prove he could do it. I quickly backtracked.

"You can do what you want, I just think it's more comfortable not in jeans. That's why I'm wearing fleece-lined leggings."

However, since we both knew he didn't have leggings, fleece-lined or otherwise, he decided to stick with the jeans. I agreed this was sensible, since the only other option was to hike naked, and we headed up into the mountains. We quickly got lost because the trail was snowed over and ended up walking in an almost perfect circle three times. An hour before sunset we turned back to avoid becoming an early bird buffet special for the ice zombies that were no doubt hanging out behind every single tree. My friend's pants were soaked to the knee. His pallor suggested one of the zombies may have already gotten to him.

This wasn't actually such a problem, because we were ultimately heading back to a car that would turn on and push hot air out of individual, adjustable vents like magic. He could remove the pants and sit naked from the butt down in my car if he wanted to, while I brought in snacks and steaming drinks and we drove mere hours back to houses with insulation and blankets and hot water. Who cares if you day hike in jeans, even in the snow?

If we had been backpacking, though, he could have died.

KNOWING YOUR FABRIC

There are four darlings in the world of backpacking fabrics: polyester, nylon, wool, and silk. And one exile: cotton.

Backpackers practically enjoy getting into arguments about the efficiency of their gear, from water filters to socks. However, there is one unanimously agreed-upon nugget of backpacking wisdom that no one debates: "cotton kills." It's less of a suggestion and more of a commandment. This is because people march happily into the backcountry wearing Levis, then they sweat or get rained on, and then they die. Seriously. Here's an example: A guy died in 2005 in the Alaska backcountry and the official report from state troopers read, "He was wearing all cotton, which is the worst fabric for cold, wet weather. The weather just got the best of him."

Cotton is extremely heavy, it chafes, it doesn't pack down, it doesn't insulate heat, and if you so much as think about water, you'll be damp for ten hours. In other words, wearing cotton is like dousing yourself in hypothermia pheromones.

Whenever I see classic footage of alpha-male, rugged cowboys—invariably in denim—galloping their horses confidently into the wilderness for a multiday quest, I can't help thinking, "Hooooow?" It works if you're a farmhand on a ranch in Arizona in 1885, but it doesn't really work anywhere else. Cotton underwear and cotton bandanas are the only exceptions to this rule, as they are thin enough to be extremely breathable and dry quickly in the sun. Otherwise: Denim is for looking like a badass. Polyester is for being one.

Polyester is the long-suffering peon of backpacking clothing. It's blended into almost everything, but rarely gets credit compared to upmarket silk, stalwart wool, and futuristic nylon. Polyester is cheap, hydrophobic (which means it naturally resists water . . . probably because it's made of oil), and stands up to tons of abuse. It's a tenth as luxurious as silk, doubly as versatile as wool, and half the price of both—but, best of all, it's probably already in your closet. Pants, shirts, socks . . . it's great anywhere on your body in the backcountry.

Nylon is kind of like polyester's older sister, who married rich. It's lighter and repels water almost as well. However, despite what I've seen people write online, in my experience it doesn't breathe. At all. You might as well wrap your legs in cling wrap and hope for the best.[9] Anyway, what nylon does do is protect you from the probing proboscises of mosquitoes, and the snags and snips of branches; its durability is unparalleled for a fabric of its weight, and it also dries quickly. This is why so many hiking pants and shirts are a blend of nylon and polyester.

On the pricier end of the spectrum, we have silk and wool. Silk is featherlight, quick- drying, breathable, insulating, and *sexy*. It's not only perfect for all your wilderness princess fantasies, it also weighs next to nothing and somehow manages to keep you cool when it's hot, and hot when it's cool. It's basically a Harry Potter invisibility cloak in the form of long johns. I dream of someday obtaining a base layer of silk.

By comparison, wool—silk's chubby Amish cousin in the natural fabrics department—is lightweight, quick-drying, breathable, and has the notable

---

9. Cling wrap is how my developmental editor's dad keeps his legs warm during cold, rain-soaked high school football games in Ohio, so I really shouldn't knock that technique.

claim of being the textile of choice for discerning outdoorsmen both before and after nylon and polyester were invented. It will keep you warmer than any amount of cotton or silk ever could—even when it's wet and cold, which makes it extremely functional for backpacking. The catch is it's nearly as expensive as silk, and also, it comes from sheep. I have this wool shirt I used to wear hiking all the time. I'd hit the trail, and after a while I'd smell sheep on the breeze, and think, "That's so cool, they're opening up pasture-land near here!" Five minutes later I'd realize I wasn't smelling the local flock, but my back sweat.

So wool's great, but only if you're hiking with someone who really loves you for you. Some people despise polyester for its ability to trap unwanted scents, even after several washings. But at least polyester smells like you, not someone else's barn.

DRESSING FOR THE WEATHER

I learned how to dress for backpacking at sixteen while in Team, the high school outdoors program I was lucky to attend. That academic year, we headed to the Sierra Nevada in October, Joshua Tree National Park in March, and Mount Shasta in May. I woke up more than once to bone-chilling cold, with a smear of ice on my sleeping bag like a glazed donut. Chuck and Patchen, our two teachers, were ultimately responsible for keeping us minors alive, and avoiding liability lawsuits, by making sure we didn't get hypothermia, frostbite, or gangrenous trench foot. That is to say, they didn't care so much if we were uncomfortable or our packs were heavy, so long as we were warm.

Thus, the clothes I brought with me on some of my first backpacking trips were as follows:

- Two sports bras
- Two pairs of underwear
- A pair of shorts
- Two polyester-blend T-shirts with permanent armpit stains
- Long underwear (top and bottom)
- A fleece jacket and some neon-purple fleece pants that made me look like the Fresh Prince of Bel-Air had an entente with a sheep

- A rain jacket that weighed as much as a cast-iron pan, and rain pants that weighed as much as a humpback whale
- Two pairs of bulging wool socks
- Two pairs of sock liners to go under them
- Camp sandals
- Boots
- A beanie
- A sun hat designed to guarantee I would be a virgin through college if I hadn't thrown it away immediately upon returning home
- Two cotton bandanas
- Polarized sunglasses

My pack weighed ninety pounds. This fact alone would give some ultra-light hikers a heart attack, but guess what? I did it. (I did it kinda slow. And complaining the whole time. Other people in my group carried just as much and complained way less. But the point is, I did it.)

Ten-plus years later, my clothing list consists of the following:

- One bra (any bra)
- Two pairs of underwear[10]
- No shorts because shorts are stupid
- Two polyester shirts
- One pair of nylon hiking pants (khaki)
- One pair of leggings (space cat)
- The *same* long underwear from when I was sixteen
- A fleece jacket or packable down jacket
- *Vastly different* rain jacket and rain pants from when I was sixteen
- Three pairs of wool-blend socks (two for hiking, one for sleeping)
- Camp sandals
- Boots
- A buff
- A beanie I will realize I forgot to pack at nine o'clock on night one

---

10. Cotton is still king here. Never sacrifice your breathability because a stranger told you a story about a guy who died in Alaska.

- Two cotton bandanas
- Polarized sunglasses

This is my basic list, and it works for most conditions. If you're going to a place where the temperature dips to around freezing at night and/or there's a reasonable chance of rain during the day, you really want that raingear and the puffy stuff. Even if it's not supposed to rain, it's still a good idea to bring your raingear, since it also provides insulation in cold and windy weather. I bring my raingear even if I think it's just barely going to drop below fifty degrees.[11] It is a twenty-ounce insurance policy against staying awake all night shivering, and I pay it gladly.

If the weather will be warm where you're headed, with zero chance of rain, you can probably ditch the rain pants and one of the jackets, and even ignore my bigotry toward shorts. If you know it's going to be cold, however, or you're not sure what weather conditions you'll be facing, just pack it all. You rarely hear anyone talking about hyperthermia in backpacking. It's hypothermia no one ever shuts up about.

To that tune, let's talk about the best way to defend against hypothermia: the layering system. You can think of it as a bit like a cake:

1. Base layer (the soft, spongy interior)
2. Mid-layer (the buttercream everyone's really here for)
3. Shell layer (fondant, which is disgusting but necessary to keep the rest of the cake safe)

Base Layer
This is just a highfalutin way of saying long johns or long underwear. The base layer sits closest to your skin and acts as the foundation of your warmth. It's also typically the layer I use as pajamas. If you're hiking in particularly cold temperatures, you can wear your long underwear beneath your regular hiking clothes to keep yourself extra warm. However, I prefer to give myself the illusion that, when I slip into them each night, they are

---

11. I was raised near San Francisco, so anything below forty-five degrees Fahrenheit is more or less the end of days.

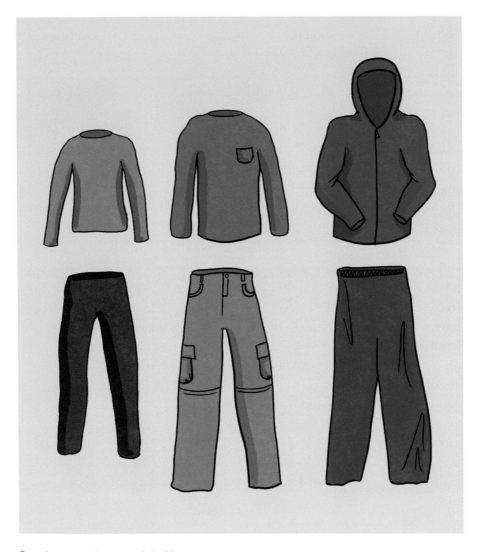

Base layer, mid-layer, and shell layer

clean, and thus I am clean, and in no way sleeping in my own filth. The reality is that after you spend a few days hiking and sleeping without showers or deodorant, your long johns will probably smell like you forever. What a friend.

Often long underwear is sold as a set, with a pullover top and the most unflattering pair of little boy pajamas you've ever seen serving as the bottoms. You'll see a lot of polyester and wool here (silk too), but these sets are pretty inexpensive—look for one that's both low price and low weight. It's generally a good idea to err on the side of what's warmer, even if you're not going anywhere cold right now, as they will be more versatile for future trips.

Mid-Layer

Chuck and Patchen never used the term "mid-layer." I didn't even learn that term until I was multiple years into backpacking. Instead, they called the mid-layer the "fleece layer," because that's what they made us wear to stay warm in the freaking tundras they took us to: a fleece jacket and a pair of fleece pants.

I need to talk to you about these pants. They were like MC Hammer pants: voluminous down the leg with snappy, elastic at the ankles, but cut from unapologetically '90s purple fleece. Think "Aladdin does Siberia." I have never seen anyone else in the backcountry wear them, before, during, or since high school. In retrospect, more than warmth, I think our teachers used them as visual cowbells to keep track of us as we ran around on rocks—shouting inside jokes and spilling soup on each other; the proud papas of a bumbling, altitude-sick, color-coordinated flock of sheep.

If I could find these pants again, I would wear them in a heartbeat. If anyone knows where they are, please write to me. However, until they turn up again, I've discovered that long underwear bottoms under a pair of my favorite unbreathable nylon pants are all I need to stay warm through the night.

Fleece *jackets*, on the other hand, are the underappreciated interns of the backpacking world. Yes, this is the same fleece jacket you see soccer moms wearing on early Saturday mornings as they schlep kids in and out of minivans. It's warm, it's light, it resists juicebox stains, and it comes in 456 colors. It's everything you want, not just in fun-but-functional motherhood attire, but also for staying dry, warm, and happy in the backcountry. The catch is, they take up a lot of room in your backpack and wind runs right through them, giving you a valuable lesson on the meaning of "windchill." So at night, when temperatures really drop into grim reaper territory, put on your long underwear top, then your fleece, and finally your waterproof jacket and tell me—just tell me—that you're not a toasty little marshmallow.

I've seen people use gossamer, lofty down jackets in place of fleece, especially the new kinds that have 900-fill down and can be mashed into the size of a teaspoon. They are disturbingly comfortable, block all the wind that your fleece lets through, and weigh mere ounces. Packable down jackets are a miracle. They are also $847.[12] If you can afford one, or borrow one, or get someone to buy you one, definitely do it. However, if you don't have a sugar daddy, cheers to soccer mom fleece.

Shell Layer

Initially, the shell layer was introduced to me as the "GORE-TEX" layer. This is because GORE-TEX was—and, I believe, still is—the gold standard fabric for waterproof clothing. The idea is that you can hike all day in the rain wearing your shell layer without getting wet and wrinkled. But here's the thing: I've never actually been dry in a shell layer. Whenever I've had to wear the full jacket and pants combo while hiking, I got so sweaty I couldn't tell where the rain started and my perspiration ended. I think there is some kind of cabal in the waterproof clothing world that won't let you become a respected designer of high-quality outdoor clothing until you advertise your fabric as "breathable," GORE-TEX included. And so this idea, that heat can vent out without rain getting in, is a lie we've all agreed to let manufacturers tell us. This, along with their hefty weight and equally hefty price tags, is probably why I've always found shell layers the most frustrating.

The plus side is that they really do keep you warm at night, especially when the wind is blowing. That's why, anytime you think the temperature might drop into the forties or below, even if you don't anticipate rain, I suggest you bring your shell layer. You'll look like the Michelin Man, and you might grow new colonies of life under your armpits, but trust me: when it unexpectedly gets cold, really cold, *scary* cold—you'll be glad you did.[13]

---

12. You might be tempted to buy a cheaper one you found on Amazon. Write to me and let me know how that goes.

13. Military surplus stores are a great, inexpensive source of shell layers. The deep irony of a flower-power liberal like me running through a meadow in army camo is not lost on anyone, but my frugality wins out over my vanity a lot.

Shell layers are designed to be roomy, so you can wear them as a shell (get it?) over the clothes you're already wearing. For this reason, it's best to size up when you purchase both the jacket and the pants. You kind of want to be swimming in them. This is not the time to say, "I bet I could fit into the [insert one size down from your normal size here]." I've done this before, and it more or less ends in you, alone on a mountain, holding pants that won't fit over your ass, having an existential crisis about the meaning of beauty while the sun goes down and you're starting to shiver. Just don't go there.

Finally, all waterproof fabrics lose their powers over time, especially if you wash them often. Since the shell layer rarely touches your skin, the good news is you shouldn't have to wash them after every trip. But when you have a piece that's been through enough trips to need a soapy bath several times, it's a good idea to touch it up. A bottle of waterproofing goo is around five dollars. I'm also pretty sure it causes cancer, but all backpackers seem to have accepted this is the price you pay for seeing wet trees.

Whatever your washing schedule, just don't put your waterproof jacket and pants in the dryer. Yes, these Herculean fabrics can protect you from epic wind, bucketing rain, and ruthless cold, but they believe the boogie man lives in your tumble dryer. Unless the tag says "I literally get more waterproof when you put me in the dryer," don't do it.

FINALLY, THERE ARE THE ACTUAL pants and shirts you wear during the day while hiking, which are never included in the venerable backpacker's layering system. This has never made sense to me. I guess some people think this is another name for base layer? Or mid-layer? It honestly depends on who you ask.

To keep myself from getting confused, I think of the above three layers as a Taxonomy of Insulation. They are what I put on at night to stay warm (until I get into my sleeping bag), and in that order. What I hike in during a typical day is entirely separate. Of course, when you get cold during the day, it's a good idea to put your fleece jacket on, and if it starts raining, naturally you should stop and put on your waterproof gear. This ensures that, no matter how hard you try to have a clean pair of "pajamas" each night, by

A NOTE ON WET CLOTHES

Don't sleep in them. Rocket science, I know, but hear me out.

After a day of hiking, it's important to take off your wet clothes and put on something dry before sunset begins. This is especially important if you're in arid weather, or up high in the mountains, where the sun can behave like a heat lamp, its life-giving heat disappearing as fast as you can flick a light switch. Whether from a dip in a lake or from collecting your sweat all day, damp clothes can turn from refreshing guards against the heat to ice blankets in a frighteningly short amount of time.

Even if you don't feel cold yet, it's important to put on your warm clothes *before* you feel any chill. Keep the heat you've earned. It's much harder to get it back once you've lost it to the night.

mile thirty, absolutely everything you own will have the heady tang of an unwashed hiker.

Finding your hiking clothes is actually pretty easy. Simply go through your drawers at home and look for some shirts, pants, and shorts that seem like they'd be easy to walk and move in. Think gym clothes and crappy Forever 21 tops (seriously). If it's comfortable, and you can move it in, it's fine. Don't feel like you have to shell out $200 for the UPF 50 T-shirt produced in collaboration with NASA. Just check the tags and make sure there's no cotton. Save your money for bigger problems. Trust me, they are coming.

EMBRACING LEGGINGS

Clothing, ultimately, is your first defense against the elements—sunburns, hypothermia, bugbites, frostbite, and all the other sticks and stones that can very much hurt you. This is Magna Mater we're talking about. Have some respect for her power. You must need some hardcore shit to take on the backcountry, right? Right.

I genuinely believe this. Which is why I have trouble justifying that nearly every time I backpack, I'm wearing a pair of leggings. And I don't mean eighty-dollar, nitro-infused, AffluEssence™ patented, control-top leggings. I mean the kind of leggings you get at lowbrow flea markets, with space-traveling toasters and fire-breathing kittens on them.

Leggings are lightweight, non-cotton, compact, designed for movement, quick-drying, and behave like a second skin—even the cheap ones. Almost all leggings are made of some variation of spandex and polyester. The only meaningful difference is whether they include a banded control top, which, for seventy dollars extra, promises you'll have to yank them up once a day instead of twice. I've hiked in ten-dollar leggings with a hole in the side, and in luxurious, designer-brand leggings with superior compression and Coolmax technology. They performed the same.[14]

You might see leggings called different things once you start exploring the world of wilderness fashion, but in my experience, the only real difference between "yoga pants," "hiking tights," and "leggings" is marketing. Generally speaking, if you can do Gandha Bherundasana in it, you can walk backward and forward in it.

The reason I'm raving about leggings is because they are actually a somewhat new tool in the backpacking community. Up until about ten years ago, the standard backcountry pant was a pair of lifeless vanilla khakis that you could barely lift your leg in. Then a few bloggers realized the pants they were downward-dogging in during yoga class would be equally nice to walk around all day in and—bam. Leggings officially entered the backpacking scene.

I can understand why some men might not feel me on this leggings obsession, but if it helps, I actually got the idea from a backpacking blog written by a man. Also, the whole idea behind backpacking is to be alone outside, away from the pitiless judgment of fashionistas and uneducated brutes who would call you a sissy. Still, I realize going about in extra formfitting bottoms isn't something society normally lets guys do. Gentlemen, I'm not gonna pretend this wouldn't be brave on your part. All I'm suggesting is that you try it. Just try it. Just around the house. If you can't

---

14. The only leggings I'd avoid are capris. Capris are like regular leggings, except with openings at the bottom that basically serve as helpful landing strips for sunburns, poison oak, scratches from sharp branches, and ticks.

handle it, that's fine. L.L.Bean is still totally down to take $100 from you in exchange for some sensible polyester khakis.

I've heard arguments against leggings. Some people assert that they are unfit for backcountry use, and that everyone should wear loose-fitting pants only—that stiffer, thicker, looser fabrics breathe better, are more comfortable, and will protect hikers better from the elements.

Bullshit. First of all, "loose pants" aren't even available to all of us.

OK, truth time? Between you and me? I have huge legs. I used to be very embarrassed about them. I remember walking into a Hot Topic in 2004 and trying on a pair of "super wide leg" black cargo pants that were *two sizes bigger* than my normal pant size. This was one in a series of attempts I made to rock the ultra-wide-leg cargo-pant goth look (if you weren't a teenager in 2004, just know that this look, and Hot Topic, were very cool). The pants were supposed to ride low on my waist, and then engulf each of my legs in a kind of denim parachute, laced with vampire chains and secret pockets. The idea was to look like a backup dancer in a TLC music video, or someone who kept bumping into Trent Reznor at clubs. However, when I put them on, instead of the voluminous skirts my legs were supposed to be swimming in, my thighs still only had one-half inch of room, at best, on either side.

I have a million stories like this. To this day, I have never been able to rock the cargo pant look, much to my extreme dismay. In 2017, when women like Ashley Graham burst out of fashion magazines screaming, "Thick thighs save lives!" I felt seen for the first time in my life.

This is why women are obsessed with leggings. Yes, it's because they are comfortable—it's also because they accept us as we are, no matter what. It's as if Deepak Chopra were a garment.

So I fight the notion that leggings are bad, because the truth is I—and a great deal of us, male and female alike—can barely walk in 100 percent nylon or polyester pants, no matter how "wide leg" they claim to be. I have ordered at least twenty different kinds of these pants online from various outdoor retailers, in as many sizes. I don't care how gusseted the knees are, or how much I size up. I need elastane or I can't lift my knee up past ninety degrees. If a bear were chasing me, and I was wearing these pants, I wouldn't be able to clamber over a single rock. Someone please explain to me how this is the safe choice in backcountry bottomwear.[15]

There is one argument against leggings, however, that holds water. Or rather, blood.

FUCKING MOSQUITOES

Mosquitoes can ruin a trip. They are like the physical manifestation of microaggressions. One or two might not bother you, but several hundred, staring you in the face twenty-four hours a day, can send you into a deep enough rage to incite a cultural revolution.

If you really, really want to avoid mosquitoes, it's best to plan your trip when they are dead or dying. In places where it snows in the winter, mosquitoes tend to be a strictly summer affair. They are born as the snow melts in spring, and then die out in the dry heat of August. By October, they are virtually gone. (Then the snow comes, like a flying grim reaper wielding ten thousand knives of ice, and annihilates them all. This is one of the most satisfying thoughts I have ever had.)

If you're worried about whether there will be mosquitoes where you're planning to go, find a book, or ask someone who has been there during the season you'll be visiting. Look online for forums, social media groups, anything. Ask the question ahead of time, and ask it specifically: "Are there mosquitoes in [place] in [month]?" Park rangers, bless them, won't always tell you.

I was well on my way to becoming a total backpackers-for-leggings evangelist, preaching from the high hills about the Wilderness Industrial Complex™ and its factory of stiff, nylon lies, and that all you need is some ten dollar leggings covered in rainbows and mermaid scales to take on any trail from Alaska to Georgia. And then I visited Crater Lake, Oregon, in July. First of all, don't ever do that. Second of all, did you know that mosquitoes can prick you straight through spandex? Also, did you know that

---

15. The actual answer here is to get nylon or polyester hiking pants with spandex blended in for movement, but they don't make those pants in space cat, so shush.

the beautiful Cascade Range, stretching from Northern California through Washington, is home to more mosquitoes than there are people on earth?[16]

I am a good girl, remember. I went to the ranger station beforehand to get information. It's generally good practice to stop by one before you head out on the trail. You can check if there are any notices about route closures or a burn ban or something else going on that wouldn't be on your map or posted online (this is very common, as the government is allergic to making information easy to find on the internet, and most people don't become park rangers because they are stoked about flawless customer UX). After entering a little office, usually peppered with flyers reminding hikers to pack out their litter and a helpful video about not feeding wildlife, I always like to ask the ranger, "Is there anything I should know before we head out?"

This ranger, who I'm sure was a nice person otherwise, looked at me like I was a kindergartner demanding extra pudding after naptime, and then gave me a twenty-minute circular lecture on "packing out what I pack in," as if I literally haven't heard it so many times I could write a book on it. What she didn't do (and should have done) is gotten a glazed look in her eyes, stared off through the nearest window, and whispered, "You will find no redemption. The little ones. They have no god."

Thus, I marched into the verdant Oregon wilderness unaware that I was functionally naked. For the next two days, I was surrounded by a gray, buzzing cloud of eager sippy straws constantly plunging into my skin. My partner had to whirl evergreen fronds around me nonstop like an energy healer just to keep the mosquitoes off long enough to pack up the tent. Upon returning to Portland, I counted 108 bites on my legs alone. Too depressed to keep counting, I slathered dangerous amounts of hydrocortisone all over my body and spent the night scratching myself like a dog under the table of a very nice restaurant. My skin was a day-old buffet. My love affair with leggings was over—that is, until I discovered permethrin.

Permethrin is an anti-mosquito and anti-tick (and anti-tons-of-other-insect-vectors) chemical that you apply to your gear and clothing, rather than your skin. You can actually buy clothes with it pre-applied, but it's also easy to treat your own clothing. Buy a ten-dollar spray bottle of the

---

16. Not a real fact.

stuff, lay out your clothes and gear outside, and spritz away while singing "Working at the Car Wash" (that last part is optional). It even lasts for a handful of laundry cycles. Permethrin is fairly new to the backpacking scene, only really becoming popular in the last few years. However, it's purported to be less toxic to mammals than other repellants (the exception being, randomly, cats, so ... you know ... don't spray it on your cat), and because you only put it on the exterior of your clothing, it makes people feel less tingly and queasy than other insect repellents. Whenever I head out into tick or mosquito country after performing this spray ritual on all my gear, the bugs float on past, maybe with a tiny backward glance, before moving on to easier targets. It's great. I wish someone were paying me to talk about this.

Before permethrin hit store shelves, there was more or less one insect repellent to rule them all: DEET. Honestly, I want to like DEET, but I have trouble bringing it into the backcountry. It's not that I'm a soft hippie who only buys PETA-approved beauty products and washes her face with vinegar and honey (although that's also true). DEET just doesn't make sense to me. It melts plastic. It says so right on the warning label on the back of the bottle. And almost all the clothing you can buy for the backcountry is made from polyester and nylon—which are made from plastic.

You're also supposed to wash it off your skin every day, because it's poison (also on the back label). But you can't wash it off in the backcountry, can you? If you want the Lorax to like you, you need to be at least two hundred feet away from any body of water (again, it says so right on the back label). The logistics of that backcountry bath are insane, and I dare anyone to tell me they are actually doing it by the Leave No Trace book. I hear backpacking bloggers that are much more hardcore and experienced than me extolling DEET as the sacred, signature ambrosia that repels mosquitos when nothing else will, but I want to ask them, "You can't wash it off your skin, and it melts your clothing, so ... how are you doing this, actually?"

If, like me, you have medical-grade sensitive skin and have heard too many propaganda speeches pronouncing all chemicals that start with D as what's killing the honeybees, there is an option to avoid chemicals altogether. The best defense against bugs, really, is your clothing, and this is where I have to concede most leggings—at least, untreated leggings—are not fit for service. Nylon is the fabric that mosquitoes have the hardest time getting through (any woven fabric will do, but since most people, myself included, can't really see the difference between a woven polyester and a knit polyester, it's easier to just say "buy nylon"). It has to do with how tightly nylon's fabric fibers come together, making it difficult for mosquitoes to stick their straws in between the fibers. Some of you might be cringing at the idea of a sunny summer day spent hiking in stuffy, unbreathable nylon, but spend a few hours as a picked-over meat platter during the mosquitoes' annual corporate retreat, and you'd hike in a spacesuit stuffed with steel wool if I told you to.

Even nylon isn't completely impenetrable though, which is why if you're going somewhere in the throes of mosquito season, it's a good idea to get at least one of the aforementioned chemicals involved. Straight patchouli and lemon eucalyptus oil also totally work according to the hippies (although the only thing you can really be sure of is that it will make you smell like the King of the Hippies).

I genuinely encourage you, gentle reader, to battle mosquitoes in whatever way you choose. The bottom line is that they are the enemy—let's never lose sight of that. They can destroy your good time if you aren't prepared. Use whatever tools you have at your disposal to get ahead of them. I support you.

PRIORITIZING FUNCTION OVER FORM

I have learned that if you tell people what to wear outside, generally speaking, they don't want to do what you say. It's not just video-game addicted men who resent being dragged outside by overeager women trying to reconnect with nature. Most people just don't like being told what to put on their bodies. They will always look for a cheaper, more comfortable, or sexier option (depending on the personality you are dealing with).

To that end, I wouldn't consider the advice in this chapter exclusive. Everyone is going to do their own thing. But the one bit of advice I'd really like to impart to you, that I have learned through many sunburns, bugbites, shivering nights in sleeping bags, and more sunburns, is that function truly matters over form in the backcountry.

When I dragged my friend into the snowy Sierra with his jeans on, hubris and lack of planning didn't really hurt anyone. He got an A+ on his self-test of suffering and manhood, and I didn't actually need to wag my finger in his face. Because the stakes weren't real. If you can return to a car well before nightfall and drive to food and shelter, the stakes are different than if you have to spend the night on the side of a mountain in cold, wet clothes. Make no mistake: this kills people.

And by the way, you don't ever need to prove you can cheat death.

Fuck the test. Fuck proving what you can handle. Health is not a dare. Be comfortable, because being comfortable is a great indicator that you are also safe. The "test" of what you can handle in the backcountry is probably coming whether you want it to or not.

If you want to drop your jacket in the lake to prove to your campmates that you are Princess Mononoke, go ahead. But be sure to dry it off for when you remember you're the primate equivalent of a bichon frise. You need your little sweater. It's cold outside.

Chapter 4

SHOES
How to Walk Upright with 15,000 Helpful Inserts

"It's a hotspot. No, it's fine. No, it's a hotspot. No, it's fine. No, it's a hotspot."
—Me

"I can't do it." My hiking poles clattered against the granite as I angrily hurled them onto the ground. I dropped like a stone thudding in the middle of the trail, letting the weight of my pack pull me down into a puff of dust. Then silence.

Amid a high-contrast landscape of electric-blue sky, jade-green scrub, and little white flowers, Jeanne and I were walking up the spine of a sky-domed canyon in Torres del Paine National Park in Chile. A glacial breeze winged past and ruffled my shirt, chilling my sweaty skin. The park is famous for its iconic mountain towers, up-close-and-personal glaciers, and ethereal streams and rock formations. It was a fairy tale in real time. I had spent thousands of dollars and was missing weeks of work to be here. Frankly, I was probably putting my career in jeopardy. But these are the sacrifices we make chasing "once-in-a-lifetime" experiences.

"I can't do it," I said out loud again, and I felt a ball of heat start to form in my throat and behind my eyes. I buried my face in my hands to hide the bright world.

"Does it hurt that bad?" Jeanne said. This was the first trip we'd taken together outside of Europe or the United States. She was also missing hundreds of dollars in work hours to be here, as well as time with her new husband.

"Yes!" I nearly screamed. It was a confession, a burst, a pressure valve releasing. I had been denying this for a few days. I didn't want what was happening to me to be happening. But we all have our limits on what we can ignore.

My right ankle was swollen; my Achilles tendon felt like a hot-pink hamburger patty. I'd taken four ibuprofens that morning, but it throbbed full force and without apology through the double dose of anti-inflammatories. At every step, my ankle creaked like a rusty door hinge, sending red tendrils of pain up my calf whenever I lifted my heel—which I'd been doing roughly nonstop since breakfast. The pain hadn't started suddenly, but actually hundreds of miles away, hiking a different trail in a different park a week earlier. In response to what was (at that time) occasional complaints and ankle massaging, our other companion, Irina—a model-faced anthropologist whom, despite severe tent claustrophobia, we had convinced to go on her first backpacking trip—rigged a handkerchief, some tape, and the underwire from one of her bras to make me a kind of cast, allowing my right foot to sit in my boot in the *one* position where I could hike carefree.

I finished that trip with remarkable ease, periodically ruminating on how to nominate Irina for a Nobel Prize in creative engineering with lingerie. But Irina had stayed behind in Santiago, and Jeanne and I went into Torres del Paine alone after a five-day break. I had thought I just needed a little rest, and that by the time we got here, my ankle would be fine. It wasn't like I was seriously injured. It was just a little shoe problem.

Now, Jeanne was standing in front of me, and I could feel her wavering between sympathy and annoyance. She didn't know what to say. What do you say to a partner whose injury doesn't quite warrant a true emergency, but hurts just enough to drag you down with them? What do you say to someone you were depending on, but who failed to do the one thing you're both responsible for—taking care of yourself first?

I tried to compose myself. "I'm not crying because it hurts. I'm sorry," I said through gritted teeth. "I mean, it does hurt. But it's not really that." Rainbows of fractured light blurred my vision as I realized the dirty truth of it. "We flew all this way, we did all this prep, we worked so hard, and this is it. This is what's gonna happen. I spent all this time making myself this vacation, this stupid nest of self-care or adventure or whatever, and I ruined it. This is the story now. I flew ten thousand miles for paradise, and I ruined it."

I sat on the ground for a few more moments, just breathing. The sun ticked an inch down toward the horizon. A white, chubby-winged butterfly bobbled past my slumped body. Life went on, oblivious to me. Eventually, the cool, gray blanket of reality fell over my shoulders. I felt a weird acceptance. I knew what was going to happen now. Whether I thought I could take it, whether I wanted to take it—or not—was beside the point. It was going to happen. I exhaled and grabbed my poles.

What would happen next was I would get up, and I would hike. I would hike for four more days on this screaming ankle. I would run into an Argentinian ultralight hiker who would smile sympathetically at my limping, clap me on the back, point to his little running shoes, and say, "That's why I don't wear boots no more!" I would also run into two middle-aged Australian nurses who would examine my pulsing ankle with maternal concern, and show me how to shorten my tendon's stretch by propping my foot up in my boot with some of their "hiker's wool" (donated by their sheep, Bobby, "who woulda been so happy to see it help yah!"). I would guzzle enough ibuprofen to question whether I'd have a functioning liver when I got back. I would wish for ice, realize I was next to a glacial lake, and then soak my foot in some of the coldest water that you could still classify as liquid. Often without asking, the full array of nature's bounty and backpacker generosity opened its gates to me. It all helped, and I was grateful. My memories of this trip are some of my best.

However, that thrumming, pulsing, stretching, screaming ankle was my companion for every step, never letting me forget that it was there, never letting me enjoy anything without it. The alternative to hiking through it, of course, was getting an emergency helicopter. But airlifts are for broken bones. Hypothermia. High-fever infections. Lung punctures.

I was just a girl in the wrong shoes.

AFTER MY TRIP TO PATAGONIA, I came home, googled my symptoms, and discovered I was suffering from Achilles tendonitis. This is a fairly common affliction for hikers and runners, but I had never heard of it until I was twenty-eight.[17] It's especially common among "weekend warriors," people who sit in an office chair most of the week and then do long stretches of fancy footwork on the weekends.

I read this once, twice, three times on different medical websites. I didn't want to accept it, because I didn't feel that "weekend warrior" described me. I went for a run two times a week, and hiked on the weekends. I had a dance class every Wednesday. How could I be a weekend warrior?

Then I realized I didn't usually run for more than forty-five-minute bursts, I never had more than an hour for a weekend hike, and my one-and-a-half hour dance classes didn't involve a lot of marching in place. How often did I spend *all day* walking, as you do when backpacking? Virtually never.

To get my ankles back to what I recognized as normal, I bought some relatively inexpensive silicone-heel inserts that I read professional soccer players used for the same problem (hey, if it's good enough for the likes of Pelé, it's good enough for me). After two weeks of minimal walking and thorough stretching, my heel felt like it was finally back to normal. To celebrate, I decided to take myself out on a short hike one Saturday morning. I stretched and warmed up my ankles, put on some supportive socks, inserted my heel cups into my boots, tied my laces, and stood. As if on command, my right ankle screamed.

I wish I could tell you I sat back down, took those boots off, marched outside, and threw them in the dumpster. I wish I could say that I had given more thought to what the Argentinian man, flitting over the rocks of Patagonia in trail runners like a happy antelope had tried to tell me about ankle support. But I didn't. I had gone my whole life under the assumption that

---

17. Cue your favorite "get ready for your thirties" jokes here.

the experts were in agreement about this one: to hike, feet need the strong, firm grasp of a boot. Plus, when I had first bought these boots in preparation for the trip to Patagonia, I took them on two break-in hikes and my ankle hadn't hurt at all. It couldn't be the boots. Instead, I assumed the pain was normal. Some part of recovery. Something I maybe even deserved, for being out of shape, or slacking.

So I kept the boots on, and I hiked—and ached. Every time I took the boots off I felt better, but I kept putting them on. I would develop Achilles tendonitis three more times, with my heel getting stronger and stronger, patiently recovering, and then screaming the minute I put those boots on again. Finally, I realized this wasn't normal. I didn't even care what normal was anymore, or if it was my fault or not.

I decided I didn't deserve to be in pain.

BACKPACKING SHOES ARE A TANGIBLE metaphor for the dangers of taking "expert" advice and ignoring what your body is telling you. Why did I insist that the problem—the reason I was in pain—was my body, not the boots? Well, first of all, I'm a woman. For many of us, it's an ancient tradition to assume that, upon attempting to insert all or part of our body into an item that clearly isn't a good fit, the wearable item is a *standard*, and we are a failing sap if we can't squeeze our bodies into it.[18] So goddamn it, we put it on anyway. This applies to everything from bras to blouses, finger rings to footwear. Most of the women you know are champions at adorning themselves in things that hurt them, then looking into a mirror with smiling, gritted teeth and saying, "this is fine."

Second, I was raised to believe suffering is a part of wearing backpacking shoes. It starts when you're a kid. You try on a hiking shoe in a store and it feels roughly as if you got your foot stuck in an IKEA bookshelf. Then your mom squeezes your toe box, and as long as there's room, she slaps the store associate on the back, pays the cashier fifty dollars, and

---

18. "Failing sap" is an understatement. It's actually that you're a gargantuan monster, destined to be banished to the barren hinterlands to live out a friendless, sexless existence until you are eventually slain by a village boy in the yearly proving ritual.

then maybe you get to stop for frozen yogurt on the way home. Whatever callouses or blisters happened after that were pretty much in god's hands until you outgrew the instruments of torture.

In high school, on my first extended (more than three-day) backpacking trip, most of my comrades and I wore stiff leather boots. After the first day, we spent half of each morning more or less mummifying our feet with various tapes, gauzes, and bandages, before plunging them into the dungeon-like recesses of our boots, lacing them up like a Victorian corset, and taking on the day.

I was taught that "breaking in" my shoes—the process of wearing them a few times before considering them ready for an expedition—removes any problems an ill-fitting shoe might cause you down the line. Pain, especially blisters, was an accepted part of this break-in process. You simply taped up your feet, and then after an arbitrary time set by no officially body (let's call it a week), the shoes were considered broken in. But, I saw again and again, even after they were broken in, that blisters still occurred if the hiking shoes were slightly too big. Or too small. Or if you just walked in them for a long time. So blisters (and, frankly, foot pain in general) were never indicators I used to tell when something was really, deeply wrong with the way a shoe fit my foot.

We are often told that pain is a teacher, but the lesson is not always straightforward. How are you supposed to know if pain actually indicates a problem you need to solve or if it's something you just need to be patient with (or if you're a weird monster for not being able to fit into something)?

Backpacking shoe advice is a maze. Some people say you should buy your shoes two sizes bigger than your normal size. Some people insist you need a boot for ankle support; others counter that boots are the cause of all ankle problems. Some people insist that if you're spending anything less than $150 you might as well flush your money down the toilet. Do you want your shoes to be waterproof or to be breathable? How much heel support do you need? Do you know how much you pronate? What's the condition of your arches?

Do you know what would happen to your feet, right now, if you immediately became eight months pregnant with twins and then decided to walk all day?

Feet are incredibly complicated. They are squishy, malformed hand flippers containing fifty-something bones and more intricate tendons and ligaments than I can name. Studying feet is almost as hard as studying the brain in medical school. Your feet are as unique as fingerprints, and way harder to care for.

One way around all this drama is to call in the professionals. Visit your friendly local foot doctor or physical therapist for an exam and recommendations. You could even check out a specialty athletic-shoe store, where I imagine you'd be greeted by an expressive old Italian man who would take detailed measurements of your foot while giving you disapproving looks over his eyeglasses, then go into the back, make a cacophony of sawing and sewing sounds, and return, smiling and holding a shoe that fits you like the glass slipper fit Cinderella the day after the ball.

This really might be worth it. When I was stretching my throbbing ankle against a rock in Torres del Paine, it occurred to me to turn to Jeanne and ask, "Wait . . . does your foot hurt?"

"Dude, I have custom inserts."

"How much were those?"

"Five hundred dollars."

I scoffed. "Are you serious?!"

She waved an imperious hand over the scene before her—my screwed-up face as I peeled my ankle off the rock, the bottle of painkillers spilling out of my pack, my hands raw from their overdependent grip on my hiking poles—and said, "I am over that shit."

Granted, we don't all have the money for custom inserts. I certainly don't. I mean, I probably should prioritize it, considering this is one of my favorite hobbies, but I also don't want to sell my kidneys.

Finding the right pair of shoes is really a lesson in trusting yourself. You have to listen to all the advice that's been given to you, and then trust your body to tell you what feels true. I hope you can get to the "trusting your body" part faster than I did. But in the meantime, here's some hard-won advice I wish someone had given me when I was first starting out.

DECIDING BETWEEN BOOTS AND TRAIL RUNNERS

For as long as I can remember, boots have been an iconic tradition of backpacking. You are going into the wild; those pampered indoor cats you call your feet need an *intense* level of protection. You need waterproof leather, kryptonite laces, unobtainium toebeds—not some spongy pair of jogging slippers!

But more and more backpackers are discovering that those flexible neon running shoes in your closet do have some serious advantages over boots. For one thing, you might already own them. They are also lighter. "One pound on your feet equals five pounds on your back" is another slice of that rare, unanimously accepted backpacker gospel, and if you ever have the option to make your back do less work, you should take it. For this reason alone, "trail runners" are quickly becoming the dark horse of backpackers' footwear. While shopping, you may see "trail runners" differentiated from "running shoes." The main difference is that trail runners have slightly beefier soles and also the marketing department needed something to do.[19]

However, there are three big reasons trail runners still hold the number two position for most backpackers. First, they aren't waterproof. Second, they don't offer as much protection against snakes and other ground hazards. Third, they offer no ankle support.

Good waterproof boots make you feel like a demigod about to take on a Hydra. They are a thick-walled, highly tractioned nest protecting your feet while the rest of your body battles the world. You can trample through streams, bushes, mud, cow pies . . . you name it. I took a tumble into some quicksand once, and my feet, snuggled in their boots, barely registered the incident. Boots are . . . *emotionally* comforting.

Waterproof boots are especially important if you're hiking in the mountains, where snowmelt and rain unite to create all manner of puddles and creeks, ensuring your water bottles shall never be dry, nor your feet either, if you aren't careful. If you're going somewhere cold and wet, let a pair of

---

19. I work in marketing—don't come for me.

waterproof boots save you from walking in sub-zero, sopping wet socks all day (which is uncomfortable at best, and can result in trench foot or frostbite at worst).

However, waterproof boots can be a double-edged sword. If you don't wear them correctly, they can trap as much moisture in as they keep out. Additionally, if you're going somewhere with streams deep enough to send water over the top of your boot, your best bet is to let the idea of "waterproof" anything go. Instead, wear something that's light, meshy, and air-dries easily (i.e., a trail runner), and walk right in.[20]

If you do this, continue to wear socks, though. Going sockless in wet shoes all day is a fantastic recipe for blisters. Just ask the eighty red boils on Jeanne's feet after she finished the Paria Canyon River Trail in Utah in a pair of sockless Keens (whereafter she refused to join me to go see The Wave, the vermillion rock formation made famous by Pink Floyd, because she, like, "couldn't walk anymore" or whatever).

Beyond water, there's also the issue of snakes. There aren't venomous snakes on every trail, but I live in rattlesnake country, so they are on my mind a lot. My heightened awareness is the result of one April day in the grasslands outside of Yosemite, when I turned a corner and my foot landed one centimeter away from the head of a sun-tanning rattlesnake (I jumped back, of course, but I am a bipedal monkey and snakes are biblical-sin Ferraris: you do the math). He did not get me, but in the mile after our encounter, I had some real time to reflect on things like my health insurance premiums, my choices in hobbies, and, above all, my footwear. If you also live in a snake-ridden area, ponder while you're picking out your shoes what would happen if you stepped on one during its afternoon siesta.

It's true most venomous snakes would rather leave you alone than bite you, but it's reassuring that boots made of canvas and leather are pretty hard for snake fangs to get through. If you're truly concerned about the risk of snakes, you should go beyond boots and get yourself a pair of snake gaiters. These are basically ballistic-grade, knee-high spats, usually made

---

20. You'll also benefit from reading a primer on how to safely wade through rivers with your pack on from an experienced trail guide. There is a distinctly right way and wrong way to do this. The wrong way can kill you.

HIKING POLES

Hiking poles (also called trekking poles) essentially turn you from a clinical anthropoid into a kind of mock quadruped. They extend from your hands down to the ground and bear (some) weight, so it's spread out over four legs instead of two. They can be extremely helpful for going both up and downhill, keeping your balance, and relieving some of the strain normally handled entirely by your knees and leg muscles. However, while some people swear by them, others find hiking poles a nuisance.

I didn't use them for years, until someone loaned me a pair to try out. I can't tell if the reason they help me go uphill is a placebo effect, or if I'm just enamored with the idea of having the option to go into a Fred Astaire cane dance breakdown whenever I want. But they are worth trying. If you don't want to buy any, you can also look for a pair of old ski poles, or just hunt around for tall, sturdy sticks out on the trail.

of canvas or leather. They'll make you look like an anime girl, so potential bonus for your cosplay game. But the bottom line is they are more effective than any pair of shoes or boots alone will ever be.

But if you're not into that look, or you're only a little concerned, you can also walk with a stick, hiking poles, or an old ski pole. If there's a snake, it'll lunge at the stick or pole, not at you. Allegedly.

Finally, aside from water and snakes, there's the confusing issue of ankle support. Too much and you'll end up mildly crippled. Not enough, and you'll end up mildly crippled. It's true that navigating through rocks, potholes, and scree offers ample opportunity to take a wrong step and give your ankle the roll of its life. Boots are superior at stabilizing your ankle, preventing it from tearing and overstretching if you happen to lose your footing. Many people prefer boots for this reason alone. However, it was a boot's aggressive "support" that partially caused all my suffering on that trail in Patagonia.

Ankle support is just like any kind of attention. It's usually great, but too much of the wrong kind can ruin your life.

DETERMINING YOUR BACKPACKING SHOE SIZE

The shoe size you wear for climbing yonder mountain is going to be markedly different than the shoe size you wear to the grocery store. The first rule I was given for buying backpacking shoes was to go up 1.5 sizes from my regular shoe size. This is to account for the combined trauma of your foot swelling under the sudden extra weight of a thirty- to seventy-pound backpack, the stress of walking all day, and the bulk of your hiking socks. It's not bad advice, and it's still advice I hear given out. But it's also advice that has never helped me. Instead, I opt to buy a half or one size larger, and a full size *wider*.[21] Why wider? Because, in my experience, when your feet swell under the pressure of excessive walking and the sudden extra weight, they do get a little longer. But mostly what they do is get wider.

I recognize this situation may not entirely apply to you. I have weird feet. I wear a women's size 11.5 wide *normally*. This is impossible to shop for; I have never met a shoe brand that believes I exist. However, even if I can't find a women's 11.5 wide, the internet does make it easy for me to find a men's 10.5 wide.[22]

To this day, whenever women ask my advice on buying shoes, I tell them to skip the "women's hiking" section of the store entirely and beeline for the men's (yes, even if you're not a She-Hulk like me). Most women wear shoes that are too narrow anyway, at least based on all the bunions I see popping out of d'Orsay flats and designer sandals on my way to work in the morning. Furthermore, men's shoes don't have the pink tax, tend to be more comfortable, and, unless you have a very petite or naturally narrow foot (or desperately need your shoes to be mauve or lavender), I can almost guarantee you'll have a better time hiking in a pair of sensibly brown dad shoes than whatever narrow, pastel-colored rat-traps they are stocking in the ladies' section. Don't be scared. They're hiking boots, not your wedding pumps. Nobody's even really gonna know, I promise.

Once you've selected a pair of hiking shoes you're interested in, it's time to try them on. To do that, you'll first need to layer on your backpacking socks, which tend to be bulkier than everyday socks. When you pull on the

---

21. You might go anywhere from a half size higher to a size and a half, honestly. Timberland translates an EU size 43 shoe as a US men's 9. The North Face calls the same EU size a US men's 10. Sizing inconsistency between brands never shows itself more clearly than in shoe shopping. If you're ordering online, make sure you get free return shipping.

22. If I was still buying women's shoes, I'd need a 12 extra wide to hike in. I don't want to get any letters about how you think my feet are weird, OK?

LET'S TALK ABOUT SOCKS

I suspect one of the principal reasons that some people still recommend purchasing backpacking shoes two sizes bigger than normal is because hiking socks used to be the podiatric equivalent of duvets. They were massive. You basically put your foot in a sheep's face and then shoved it in a shoe. And sometimes you would get liners (thin polyester slip socks) that you would put on UNDER your billowing wool socks, further engorging the whole affair. Pair this with the moleskin, tape, and bandage collage most hikers paint on their feet at the start of each day, and not only is it amazing any of us got through a morning without ladies-in-waiting, but as far as our shoes could tell, our feet nearly doubled in size.

Today, wool-blend socks, which are positively lithe in comparison, have swept the market. There is a reason these socks, typically made of 70 percent wool, 28 percent nylon, and a touch of spandex, have become something nearly all backpackers agree upon: they are lightweight, quick to dry since they don't contain any cotton, incredibly durable, easy to wash, and suitable for both hot and cold weather.

However, even these modern wool-blend socks are thicker than your regular Tuesday-at-the-office socks, and this can actually make a huge difference in how your foot fills a shoe. It's like trying on a coat in a fitting room stall while wearing a T-shirt, and then attempting to put it on over a cable-knit sweater in front of your mother-in-law on Christmas. Set yourself up for success. Try on your intended shoes with your intended socks to ensure you're buying the right shoe size.

potential shoes-to-be, don't crank the laces down to death; just tighten them as you normally would with your other shoes. Since you're sizing up, they might feel a little loose. You want them to feel friendly, but from a respectful distance—like you're on an internet date with a guy who obviously really likes you, but is smart enough to know that you just met an hour ago, and he shouldn't be giving you that two-hand-butt-squeeze girlfriend hug just yet.

Now stand up and take a few steps. Is your heel lifting up and out of the boot when you walk? This is generally to be avoided, as it causes undue stress on that precious, precious Achilles tendon. You can try lacing the straps a bit tighter, but it also might be a signal you need a shorter or narrower footbed (i.e., a different boot). Take a few steps to feel this out. Then, stop in front of something you've been wanting to kick for a really long time, like a 1990s inkjet printer, or a picture of the Keystone XL Pipeline. Go ahead and kick it (maybe a few times).

Did your toes hit the front of the shoe? If they did, they will also hit the front of the shoe when you're walking downhill. That's fine for a little bit, but after an extended period, your toenails will revolt, give you the finger, and fall off. You'll need to go up another half or full size.

BREAKING IN YOUR NEW SHOES

You know how we spent all that time talking about how your body is your voice of reason and the importance of listening to your instincts and all that shit? Well this part is still gonna hurt, probably, and you're still not supposed to read into it. It's like a first meeting between your foot and this new thing you're forcing it into an arranged marriage with. They are bound to rub each other the wrong way at first. This is why blisters and some discomfort are considered acceptable.

There isn't a standard amount of time it takes to break in your new shoes, but more is better. The good news is that you probably had hiking on your agenda anyway, as the best way to prepare for a backpacking trip is to go on as many day hikes as possible. Whether it's four miles, eight miles, or twenty miles, grab a friend and make a day of it, if you can.

I realize not everyone's schedule allows for numerous obligation-free days of skipping through the woods, but a few weeks of hiking some laps around the city park after work will accomplish the same thing. Your boots might not match anything you wear at the office, but a fashion faux pas is a small price to pay for the alternative. If I had taken my new, high-quality, backpacker-approved, Vibram-soled boots on more than two sixty-minute hikes before I took them out on a multiday backpacking trip, there's a very good chance I would have known what was coming, and I could have walked, rather than limped, through one of the most iconic backpacker paradises in the world. But I didn't. Be better than me.

If the first date between your feet and your shoes appears to be sliding downhill fast after a few miles—your shoes gripping your feet like a vise or a ring of fire popping up around your toes—it's probably an indicator that this break-in needs to turn into a break-up. It's a real bummer when it happens because you can't return shoes after you've worn them outside, right? Well . . . usually.

There are at least two places where you can buy shoes, get them fucking filthy, and then get all your money back if you decide "actually, I changed my mind." This is why I still think of REI and L.L.Bean, despite the snobbery and eye-popping price tags, as corporations ultimately powered by all the love and understanding you never received as a child. Don't let anyone know I told you.

DEALING WITH BLISTERS

On my very first backpacking trip, when I was fifteen, my mother told me to look out for "hotspots." This is when a section of your foot starts to feel, well, hot as you walk. The heat is actually the result of a friction burn as a little spot on your skin starts to rub against your shoe a smidge too eagerly. "If you feel a hotspot, stop and put a Band-Aid on it," my mother cautioned helpfully as we were lacing up our boots that morning. "If you don't, it will turn into a blister, and those are much harder to deal with."

The thought of hiking with a blister—a fragile, icky bubble of pain that could release its goo at any moment—scared me so much that every other minute I was convinced I felt something heat up in the dark mystery of my footbed. "It's hot! It's hot!" I would squawk. Each time I did this, my mother would patiently stop, drop her pack, gently undo my boot, take off my sock, and put an adhesive bandage on what threatened to be a boo-boo. I would then roll my sock back up and lower my foot back into my boot with the same care one usually reserves for disarming bombs.

I adapted this tactic, after the second or third stop, when I realized that if I wasn't careful with how I put my shoes and socks back on, the bandage would quickly stop adhering to my sweaty skin. This left me walking in a kind of neurotic stupor, unable to focus on anything but the feeling of the adhesive bandage gently tickling the side of my foot, unable to figure

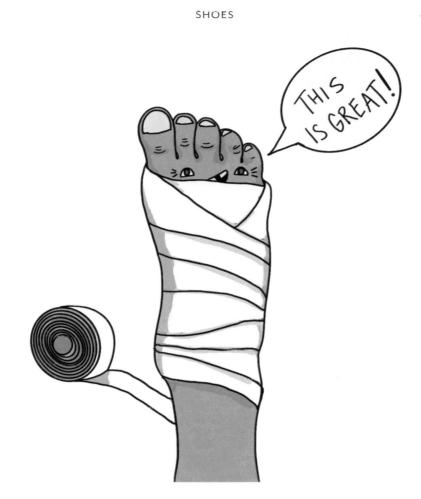

out if it had fallen off or was still in place.[23] Meanwhile, I could feel over there, just there (I swear!), another hotspot forming. By the fifth time we stopped, my mother was still helping me, but also sighing in a way that suggested she was remembering the impressionability of children. Eventually each foot was covered in so much tape and gauze and moleskin that I looked like a surgery patient. Little pieces of my foot peeked out through the wrappings, as if to wonder what the hell was going on out there. We had been hiking for an hour.

---

23. In ancient cultures this is a noted form of torture.

Since then I have learned a lot about blister management, and if we're being honest with each other, it's just about the only thing in this book I feel utterly confident talking to you about. First off, accept that blisters are inevitable. Bad shoes will cause more, while good shoes will cause fewer, but if you're moving your feet all day for days on end, you're likely to get at least one. A lot of experienced hikers will claim they don't get blisters, but I've never fully believed them. I think they just have callouses—blister sites so worn over by repeat offenses they've lost sensation. Still, I'm happy to say that after years of suffering, my blisters are rare enough to be a surprise. Usually, sometime on day three, I'll take off my shoes and socks in preparation for a refreshing soak in a crystalline creek, and discover there's a tiny stowaway on my pinky toe. "Oh hello, little asshole. Glad you could join us."

If you find yourself with a blister in the wild, there are a few methods of dealing with it.

Adhesive Bandages

The standard-issue treatment for a minor boo-boo, adhesive bandages work well when their sides are taped down. Otherwise they just kind of wiggle around in your shoe in a way that still, fifteen years later, drives me to the brink of madness. I don't like that feeling, but hey, everyone gets off in different ways.

Moleskin

Moleskin is a thick, pudgy type of gauze—like if some khakis and a bowl of Jell-O had a baby. It's typically sticky on one side, so you can slap it on a hotspot, or, if you already have a blister (especially a big one), you can cut a hole in the moleskin and then put it around the blister, like a frame for your suffering. This prevents the fragile skin of your blister from rubbing up against your shoe, without putting any adhesive over it.

At least, that's the idea. This is advice I've heard, but it has literally never worked for me. Moleskin is thick, but it's not that thick. The last time I got a blister, framed it in moleskin, then put my shoe back on, my blister laughed, thanked me for the exposure, exploded, and created a disgusting mess in my shoe.

But that is just my feet. Maybe yours will get along great with moleskin.

Medical Tape

Transpore medical tape was a staple in my house when I was growing up.[24] My sisters and I used to beg my mother to buy us elegant, smooth ribbons of Scotch tape for our school projects and Christmas presents, but we were frequently pointed toward the Transpore under the sink instead. We used it on everything, from hanging up posters in our rooms to fixing small electronic devices and, in a pinch, on wounds. When I got in a fender bender at age eighteen and my car's headlight popped out, the obvious solution was to reattach it to my bumper with medical tape. So when I found the Transpore in the bathroom cabinet while packing a medical kit for my first backpacking trip, it seemed like a very natural thing to take along. As far as I was concerned it was the Swiss Army knife of sticking.

Transpore tape is like Scotch tape, but covered in that gritty veneer you see on cheap plastic water glasses in diners. Transpore is also stronger and wider, and you never have to use your teeth to rip off a section—it comes off in clean, even strips using just your fingers. In truth it is wonderful stuff for backpackers' feet: sticky enough to stay firmly on your foot all day but gentle enough not to rip the fragile, lilywhite face of a blister. It's also useful for holding down gauze over other minor wounds (which is, I think, its actual intended function). For a long time, I was a huge proponent of carrying a tiny, weightless roll of Transpore tape into the wilderness as the tool for any job.

Then I discovered gaffer tape.

Gaffer Tape

Gaffer tape is duct tape that went to finishing school. It's typically used in professional photography and industrial theater work, but I think it's the best thing to happen to backpacking since beef jerky. It's a thick, fabric-backed tape that's easy to rip with your fingers, bends like a wisp of silk, and sticks like superglue, but at the same time, it is disturbingly easy to remove. If you put it on your foot, whether on a hotspot or on a blister, you can't feel anything through it—it's like you've suddenly grown a layer of X-Men superskin.

---

24. It's a thing that happens when your mom is an ER nurse.

But the best thing about gaffer tape is its versatility outside of your medical kit. When my nylon pants got in a fight with a log in the Ventana Wilderness on California's central coast, I patched the hole with gaffer tape. My old tent bottom sprung a ten-inch rip in its floor seam after a camping trip outside of Bakersfield, and it is still waterproof—after *two years*—because of gaffer tape. If the soles of your shoes came loose from the uppers, gaffer tape could probably hold them together. I think the only thing it can't do is your taxes.

Instead of lugging a gigantic role of drama kid tape on your trip, you can wrap a few loops onto a hard-sided water bottle, or even just around itself in a ziplock bag (so it doesn't get dirty). Gaffer tape can be tricky to find in regular outdoor retail and hardware stores; you might have better luck at an art supply or musical equipment outlet. It's worth the extra trip.

Lancing

If you get a blister, it's best to treat it like a baby. This means not shaking it, poking it, prodding it, or even draining it. Just swaddle it and try to make it comfortable.

If it's bigger than half an inch, however, and you sense it will explode in your shoe if you try to Ferberize it, this is one of those rare case where lancing is a good idea. You squeamish folks can skip the rest of this section, but for everyone else, here is a step-by-step guide to lancing a blister in the wilderness:

1. Don't.
2. If you really, really, really can't follow step one, grab a needle.
3. Realize you didn't bring a needle, because you didn't bring a sewing kit, because someone told you all you needed was gaffer tape.
4. Grab your knife.
5. Wash or apply hand sanitizer to your hands as thoroughly as possible, without getting soap into an open body of water.
6. Wash or apply hand sanitizer to the skin around the blister as thoroughly as possible—again, without getting soap into an open body of water.

7. Clean your knife of any debris with at least water, but preferably soap and water, and run it through fire (from your lighter, preferably, to avoid soot) to sterilize it as much as possible.

8. Gently tip the point of your knife into the top of the blister. Create the smallest hole possible for fluid to drain out of.

9. If your skin is still wet with hand sanitizer, scream.

10. As the fluid drains, meditate on the fact that you now have an open wound on your foot, and the interior of your shoes could be fairly described as a horny bacterial frat house.

11. Once the fluid has drained, apply a bit of antibiotic ointment, if you have it. Then, cover the blister in either an adhesive bandage or sterile gauze (i.e., gauze that you just took out of a sealed package). Tape either of these options down.

12. At the end of each day, undo the dressing, take a look at how the blister is healing, wash it, and let the wound air-dry for a bit. Apply a fresh, clean dressing before putting your shoes back on each morning.

13. Once the skin over the wound is solid, and nothing feels tender, consider yourself healed. Feel free to walk without the dressing, but keep an eye on it, as blisters like to form in the same place twice. If you're lucky, you'll develop a callous. If you're unlucky, another blister. If you're cursed, an infection.

CARING FOR YOUR FEET

There are worse things that can happen to your feet than blisters, but many of them can be prevented through basic hygiene and grooming. For example, it's a good idea to clip your toenails before you hit the trail. This is actually really important, even though the reason why isn't obvious unless someone explains it to you.

Consider my boyfriend—my calm, generous boyfriend, a man who had trusted me to show him the ropes on his first backpacking trip—sitting alone in his bathroom, slowly peeling his purple, blood-streaked toenail off its bed (or so I imagine—he wouldn't let me in to watch). It had been wiggling around for two months, ever since a trip to Big Sur that involved several miles of steep downhill, each step of which slammed his front toes into his boots. He did size his shoes up, but unlike most men who identify as "lumbersexual," he forgot to get his regular mani-pedi before trudging into the woods that weekend. So as far as the front of the boot was concerned, his foot had simply gotten longer from when he first tried them on in the store.

His toenails were having none of it. Your toenails are alive, and like all self-respecting living things, if you abuse them long enough, they will eventually want nothing to do with you. At the end of the day, we took our boots off and huddled in the tent, staring in fascination as his toes blushed shades of aubergine and magenta you typically only see in Renaissance oil paintings. These bruises had formed as his toes slammed into his shoes over and over, warning of things to come.

My boyfriend is a patient man. He had been looking forward to his first backpacking trip, trusting me completely to teach him everything he needed to know to stay safe and comfortable along the way. Not to make it about me, but it really made me feel bad when I found out he had to rip off his own toenails because of my incompetence.

My goal is to not let this happen to you. Clip your toenails before you head out.

But there's more to backpacking foot care than foreplay. Just like after any good session of deliberate abuse, you'll want to ensure your feet get proper aftercare at the end of their Mr. Gray–themed date with the trail.

If you find your feet are peeling excessively, or have a particularly bad odor, you may have developed athlete's foot. While you should address it, athlete's foot is really not that uncommon among, well, athletes (you went backpacking—you count as one of them now), so there's no need to panic. On the single occasion I've had athlete's foot, a foot soak in a basin of white vinegar at home cleared it up in one shot. However, if you're not into hippie home remedies, you can simply grab an over-the-counter cream. On the trail, where you won't have access to either vinegar or a pharmacy, sometimes a little fresh air, a dip in a creek, and the afternoon sun are all your feet need to feel like themselves again.

Above all, be sure to listen to your feet when you're out there. Give them space, air, and clean socks to sleep in at night. They are the indicator species of success; the fate of everything rides on their happiness. Treat them—and by extension, yourself—with the necessary respect, and you'll do great.

Chapter 5

SHELTER
Bury Yourself Alive
in Hot Green Nylon

"This pop-up tent is so easy to put back in its case."
—No one ever

I'm going to tell you something absolutely no one wants to admit: the most critical item on your backpacking gear list is your tent. Some people will sensibly argue that the stove is the most critical (because it can cook your food and sanitize your water), or your map (because it can get you home safely), but they are wrong. It's not that tents protect you—although they are an excellent barrier against things like rain, snakes, and those flies that always seem to aim for your eyes and nose. No, tents are about psychology. If you were to anthropomorphize all your gear, your water purifier would be a stalwart chemistry professor, lawfully concerned with your safety and well-being in a clinical—if not entirely huggable—way; your sleeping bag would be a fussy nanny, warming you up through a clucked barrage of "I told you so" for staying out so late. And your tent would be your mom.

At the end of day one on your journey—lavender glow lighting up the mountain face, cool scent of twilight exhaling from the rocks and trees, all of nature seeming to stretch its arms and prepare for a restful sleep— something inside of you will start to tremble. You will not take in the majesty of this precious moment. Instead, slowly, you will be overcome by the sensation that something is off. Very off. This sensation is your subconscious doing a specific calculation: the rate of incoming darkness, divided by your geographic distance from friends, qualified adults, priests, or Dwayne "the Rock" Johnsons. The math does not look good.

This feeling is normal, the result of millions of years of evolution. Your prehistoric lizard brain, armed with a toolbox of prudent, defensible instincts that got our species where we are today, is attempting to tug on your sleeve and tell you that, with each dimming gradient of light, you are losing your status as "top of the food chain" and approaching the territory known as "fucked."

In this first, most tender of panics, it is your *tent* that's going to rescue you. A magical contraption of metal tubes and whisper-thin nylon. Nylon? Nylon. You remember nylon. Synthetic, invented in a civilized laboratory by civilized men and women in white lab coats who yell at interns and drink their coffee black. They have created this for you, for your protection. And now it is time to use it.

Pitch your tent and crawl in. Lay out your pad and fall into the warm, squishy arms of your sleeping bag. Observe the light as it cascades through your new neon cocoon. You have walls. You have a ceiling. The chirping of the birds outside is unmuffled, but the mosquitoes, like a band of cockney orphans who knocked at the door and found themselves at the mercy of your English butler, cannot get inside. A warm feeling washes over you as your muscles unclench. You're going to be fine.

The psychological trick of how a big swath of pantyhose fabric, held up with aluminum twigs and Boy Scout Velcro, can feel like a nuclear bomb shelter is one of the greatest mysteries of "communing with nature." Nevertheless, my advice is to not overthink it. Ignore your skepticism and allow yourself to feel that the tent is protecting you from bugs, bears, demons, avalanches, hail, rain, and guys who want to make a dress out of your skin (even though it only protects you from three of those things). This lie is what's going to get you to sleep tonight. And you need your strength. Tomorrow is a busy day.

SELECTING A TENT

Because there are so many different kinds of tents out there, with outrageous prices and marketing that sounds like advertising copy for a freshly minted Marvel superhero, I want to cut through the fat. I don't have any brands to recommend (although I will gladly take sponsorships, if any marketing execs are reading this). If you are purchasing a tent, whether new or used, there are three main factors to consider: shape, weight, and seasonal rating.

There are two main ways to go about getting a tent on the cheap:

1. Find a friend who owns a tent, and go backpacking with them.
2. If that's not an option for you, try looking for used or clearance tents. Fall is the best time to find deals. Craigslist often has listings pop up after Burning Man, while shops usually hold sales as America's camping season dies down and they start clearing out inventory to make room for parkas and snow boots.

Shape

Tents come in many fascinating geometric shapes. Some tents are sleek "easy open" domes that pop from 2D to 3D with a flick of the wrist. Others have seven tiny poles with locking chevrons that form a kind of flaming-neon sarcophagus. In my experience, both of these are headaches waiting to happen. I prefer instead to use the standard-issue X-frame tent, which are perfect for 95 percent of all your backpacking needs. Tents with more complicated shapes will likely perform better in violent amounts of wind and rain, but unless you're planning to summit K2, they're generally not worth the effort they take to set up or the weird configurations they force you to sleep in.

The pop-up tent has recently emerged as an overcorrection to the problem of overcomplicated backpacking tents, promising to save us from the

Upper left: simple backpacking tent; lower right: a divorce waiting to happen

anguish of sliding poles into slots ever again. It's true, opening a pop-up tent lives up to its promise of "ultra-easy set up." However, getting a pop-up tent *back* in its case is about as easy as getting a genie back in the bottle, so unless you're Larry Hagman, stick with your X-frame.

X-frame tents are basically pyramids. They have two poles, one tent body, and require little knowledge of advanced geometry. You lay out your tent completely flat, push the poles through the tubes in the shape of an X, raise it up, stake it down, and you're done. It's extremely satisfying. Raising a functional shelter with this little effort in this little time is the closest I have ever come to feeling like a wizard.

Weight

As potentially the heaviest item you'll carry, weight is *the* factor when it comes to tents. As such, try to aim for something under ten pounds. And this is being extremely generous. In fact, if you meet someone on a trail and tell them your tent weighs ten pounds, they'll probably laugh so hard they'll fall off a cliff. (In which case you can harvest them for dinner. But that's no good, because you need to eat the food you brought in order to make your pack lighter, because you've already wasted ten precious pounds of pack weight on your tent.)

I say ten pounds because I have backpacked with a ten-pound tent and lived to tell the tale. I was twenty and broke, it was fifty dollars, and honestly, it didn't ruin my life. It was heavy, but stuffing it into a compression sack shrunk it convincingly. However, it would be abject idiocy for me to recommend that you use a tent that heavy. Under five pounds is standard for most backpacking tents. Anything that weighs more than that and calls itself a backpacking tent is just trying to trick you. (And this happens a lot. I am literally staring at an advertisement for a ten-pound Coleman Sundome "backpacking tent" as I'm writing this.)

Regardless of how much it weighs, it's generally good form to split up portions of the tent among the members of your backpacking team (for instance, one person carries the poles and the rain fly, while the other person carries the main tent body). This division of weight is a good way to ensure that everyone is carrying their fair share and that you never lose your entire tent in one go—for example, if the person carrying the poles flings their pack into an abyss, you'll still have the nylon tent body to wrap their corpse in after you kill them for losing the poles. If, for any reason, you do volunteer to carry the entire tent, make sure you are not also saddled with the bulk of the food. If you find yourself carrying both for your group, this is not an indicator that you are Mr. Universe; rather, it's an indicator that you should get better friends.

Seasonal Rating

Unlike the objects you tend to swipe right on during a normal cold weather cuffing season, most tents are designed for shacking up in spring, summer, and fall—the primary backpacking seasons. This is what is meant by "three seasons" in gear advertisements. The fourth season is winter. No one ever really talks about winter. If the backpacking seasons were at a high school party, winter would be the icy prep school kid, dressed vaguely like a vampire and hanging out alone in the back (if you go talk to him, he'll tell you himself he's saving "his gifts" for the especially wealthy and masochistic).

Even if you like the idea of snow camping, I wouldn't recommend it as your first trip. Winter camping is a death cult. The ground is either slippery ice or powder that may or may not suck you down ten feet into the underworld, your maps don't work because the trails are buried in feet of snow, and if you fall into water you die. You can't even take your hands out of your gloves for too long because they will turn black; the air is poison, for fuck's sake. I'm not saying never do it. Snow camping can be fun if you dig the idea of sunburning the inside of your nostrils while frostbite devours your pinky fingers. I'm just saying give yourself a few rounds with the spring nymphs before you party with the vampires.

All that said, if you find yourself with a budget of over $500 and you're into ice play, consider buying a four-season tent over the cheaper three-season. They will be heavier, but they retain exponentially more heat, and this is a good thing ("I'm too hot in here" is a sentence rarely uttered by backpackers anywhere outside of the equatorial line). Four-season tents also tend to last longer and put up with more abuse. If you have the means, go for it and get one. However, if you don't have any intention of camping in the snow, save yourself the weight and the money, and get a three-season tent. They're fine. Really.

ASSEMBLING YOUR TENT KIT
The anatomy of a proper tent kit is as follows:

- Tent body
- Poles
- Stakes
- Tarp (unless your tent bottom is already made of tarp, or otherwise reinforced)
- Rain fly
- Compression sack or other bag in which to put tent

The tent body, the nylon balloon that you drape over the poles, is the biggest part of this whole kit. Somehow, despite the fact that it can balloon up to something big enough to fit two or more exhausted heaps of humans,

it has the magic power to smoosh down to a tenth, twentieth, or even a fif-
tieth of its expanded size. This is especially true if you employ a compression sack for the smooshing.[25]

The poles provide structure for the tent body. They are usually a bundle
of hollow sticks connected by an elastic string running through them. It's a
rather satisfying game to click and snap the pole segments together, but play
gentle. Think of the poles as a spine. If the outer bones break, they can be
repaired. If the inner cord snaps, it's probably not going to stand up anymore.

The stakes hold your tent down—they look a bit like miniature Little
Bo-Peep sheep crooks but are made of stainless steel. You loop the crook
end through the little tabs on the four corners at the bottom of your tent,
and then stab the earth with the other end. A friendly rock can work to
pound them into the ground.

A tarp is exactly what you are thinking of when I say the word "tarp." One
of those crinkly, blue-gray sheets that you see large men tugging down over
truck beds or lifting up to reveal a pile of firewood. Tarps are also known as
footprints, but the difference is that footprints cost seventy dollars, while
tarps are ten dollars. They do the same thing: sit under your tent and protect its delicate nylon bottom from getting scratched up.[26] Some tents have
a built-in tarp bottom (which I am a huge, huge fan of). But, if yours does
not, you should pick up a small tarp (as close to the dimensions of your
tent bottom as you can get) from any hardware store. Tyvek HomeWrap
works extremely well too. Just get a cut off a big roll, and then snip it to fit
the dimensions of your tent floor. Either solution will compact down well
enough, as long as you really believe in yourself. If getting a special sheet for
your tent to lay atop feels too much like gilding the lily, you can ignore me.
See if I care if your tent floor gets shredded by rocks when you roll around in
the middle of the night. (I lied. I care so much about you. Please get a tarp.)

A rain fly seems useless until you're caught in a storm without one.
Most tent bodies are made partially of sheer mesh, which lets air in and

---

25. Smooshability is typically correlated to price, but it is magnificently satisfying to watch your
outdoor bedroom pack down to the size of a sandwich baggie.

26. Is nylon durable or delicate? It honestly depends on who's trying to sell you something.

keeps bugs out. The rain fly drapes on top of the mesh to actually keep out the weather. It's important. When I was fifteen and my mother took me on my very first backpacking trip to Yosemite in June, we stayed at low elevations, on a thin slice of a trail that wandered through abundant, flowering meadows and low-hanging trees. The first night out, we pitched our tent, made some dinner, chatted a bit under a sky the color of bluebells, and eventually went to sleep.

Some hours later, snuggled deep in my bag, I awoke to the pitter-patter of raindrops on our tent roof. Half-asleep and, like most girls, prone to associate this sound with cheery winter nights curled under cozy blankets holding steaming mugs of tea, I drifted back to sleep.

After an indeterminate amount of time, I woke up again. Sitting bolt upright, I shouted, "OH MY GOD! Mom! Mom! It's raining! All our stuff is outside! We're getting soaking wet!" I began to scramble out of my sleeping bag in a panic.

My mother didn't roll over. "Yeah, I know. I got it," she said groggily.

I looked around in the shadows as shapes slowly morphed and came into view. I realized I couldn't see the treetops above us anymore; suddenly I sensed I was under a very low ceiling. Our gear—packs, boots, and all—was nestled under the rain awning outside. While I was drooling in a *koselig* stupor, my mother had gotten out of bed, unzipped the tent, located our rain fly, flung it over her ungrateful heap of a daughter, stowed all our precious items under the rain fly to protect them from damp ruin, and gone back to bed. Now, five minutes later, I'd awoken to take control of this situation. I blinked.

"Thank you," I said. I lay back down and vowed to buy her peppermint foot lotion when we got back to civilization.

SETTING UP YOUR TENT

Like my mother and me on our first backpacking trip together, you will be faced with two temptations after the daylong hike to your campsite: to skip setting up the rain fly and to not bother staking down your tent.

You will be tired. You will probably be hungry. You will have certainly started to think this whole thing was a bad idea. However, you must not give in to the aforementioned temptations. Granted, if it is already raining,

THE WONDERS OF DUCT TAPE

Tents are designed to be tough, but nothing is invincible. You might notice that your new tent came with a repair kit, containing various glues and wands and patches, so if it takes damage in a fistfight with a rock, or gets into an especially tough political argument with the forest floor one night, you can return the tent to its original glory. However, to me, "repair kit" is a synonym for "duct tape."

Duct tape can mend holes in tents, reinforce failing waterproof seams, fix a boot, patch a hole in your pants, and protect a blister on your foot. Gaffer tape, duct tape's fancy cousin, is even better, if you can find it. Honestly, if you asked me to pick between a Swiss Army knife and duct tape, I would pick duct tape. It's basically a gentleman's butler, but for backpackers.

or very windy, common sense won't give you any choice but to use your stakes and rain fly. But maybe it's not raining. Maybe you've lazily shrugged your pack down and are stretching out like a lizard on a hot rock, the sun melting you into soft, golden butter as you savor the celestial, stoned feeling brought on by exercise endorphins and unfamiliar blood-oxygen levels. Do you really need the fly? The sky looks fine. The weight of your bodies will hold the tent down, right? Right. You'll be fine . . .

No. That's the high talking. Be vigilant. This is your moment.

If you're backpacking with a buddy, a division of labor usually starts to occur once you decide to make camp: one of you begins cooking, while the other sets up the tent. If you are on tent duty, don't take shortcuts. If it rains in the middle of the night, and all your stuff (that is, your backpacks, boots, socks, shirts, underwear, sleeping bags, food, and maps) gets wet because you didn't put up the fly, your backpacking partner is allowed to murder you. This is their right, and it holds up in court. Don't risk it. Just put up the rain fly.

Staking your tent is as important as putting up the rain fly, although the reasons for it can seem even less obvious. One of my first backpacking teachers told me a story about a couple who had hiked into Joshua Tree National Park during a whipping windstorm. They set up their tent, and before they could even so much as toss a sleeping bag inside, it merrily blew up into the sky. I know it doesn't take a physics major to deduce that high wind + weightless nylon bubble – tether to the earth = flight, but this equation can solve itself faster than you can blink. So up the little tent flew, lazily twirling in the jet stream like a free advertising blimp for Kelty. The campers stared upward in slack-jawed mortification. Then they began to follow it. What else could they do? It was March in Joshua Tree—sudden downpours were common. They wandered into the cactus and scrub, chasing a kite without a string. I heard they found it about seven miles later, snoozing happily in a tree.

Stories like this are more common than you think. Maybe you believe you can move faster than these poor saps, that all they needed to do was put some weight in the tent. However, even after you've tackled the element of air by adding weight to your tent, you still have to contend with water.

You know how sleds work? How, even though you're heavy, a little push can send you gliding over the snow? Tents can slide across the earth, too, if there's enough water beneath them (say, from a sudden rainstorm) and especially if there's a little wind to push them. You don't want to wake up at two in the morning, realize you are actively sliding off a cliff, and have your last thought be "I really should have staked down my Happy Sunshine Skydome two-person tent."

I know staking your tent seems redundant given all the weight you'll be putting inside it. But one day, it won't be. One day you'll wake up in the middle of the night in what feels like the second coming of Noah's flood and fall right back asleep, comforted in the knowledge that your home is safely tethered to the earth. In the morning, you'll be dry, warm, and in the same place you put your head down the night before.

Finally, my last piece of tent advice is to practice setting yours up before you head out. Actually, that should be my first piece of advice, or, potentially the only piece of advice I give you about tents at all. It's fairly important that you know, intimately, how your tent works, and that you have all the necessary parts to make it work *before* you hit the trail. You do not want to discover that you are missing a pole or that you mistook an ironic 1980s windbreaker for a rain fly when you're at 7,000 feet.

You can practice in your backyard, if you've got one, but if you are an average American twentysomething that doesn't have a backyard—maybe you have a shitty three-bedroom apartment that you share with seven strangers from Craigslist, which is why you are itching to go backpacking in the first place—don't worry: just set up your tent in a park. Or at a friend's house, or in the living room, or at night in the middle of your street. Honestly, wherever, just figure it out and set up your tent. Everyone will stare at you while you do this, but this process is important because the next time you do it, you'll be tired, cold, cranky, and possibly out of flashlight batteries, and that's not a great mindset for learning.

Soon you'll be able to set up your tent with your eyes closed. You'll be the keeper of your very own portable hearth and home. In fact, this might be the closest you'll ever get to buying your own home, because you're underwater in student loans, and you just spent all your money on backpacking gear. So really savor it.

SLEEPING WITHOUT A TENT

More experienced backpackers may be aghast at the recommendations in this chapter, thinking, "Psssh, one time in Yosemite, I saw John Muir's ghost and he told me to drop-kick my tent into the Tuolumne River. I've slept outside ever since and I'm fine." Good for you.

I have seen tons of backcountry "shelters" devised by people who insist tents are heavy, outdated, and inefficient. They extol the benefits of their chosen post-tent solution. For example, the "tarp between two trees" method, which involves tying a rope between two trees, draping a tarp over it, staking the tarp down to create a roof, and sleeping under it. This seems like an appropriate solution for keeping rain off your gear while ensuring every cold breeze catches you in a vise grip, and every willing mammal can walk right up and give your crotch a good sniff in the middle of the night.

Another alternative is the hammock. Oh my god, I love the idea of a hammock. You carry a fistful of cloth, paracord, a large sheet of mesh, and carabiners in your pack, then, when you make camp, you simply lash the cloth between two trees using the paracord and carabiners, climb in like a baby kangaroo, and lay the mesh over yourself like a death shroud. I desperately want to try this. (I'm being serious.) What has deterred me is that I'm never certain I'll end up in a place with two trees the perfect distance apart for a hammock. In my experience, nature rarely serves up such perfect accommodations, especially if you like to hang out above the tree line. I have a feeling I would end up sleeping on the ground, with no sleeping pad (because I didn't bring one, as I was supposed to be swinging between trees in island bliss every night). Also, I'm not sure crotch-sniffing mammals are deterred by hammocks, either.

Finally, there are those who refuse to let anything come between them and the stars. They're unafraid of what might bite them in the face, and they dream confident dreams in which there are no snakes, scorpions, or low-pressure weather patterns ready to batter their unconscious bodies.

I have never heard of a backpacker who, when told of someone else's shelter, said, "That's a great idea. I have no ideas or suggestions as to how you could improve that system." Along with boots versus trail runners, how you protect yourself from bugs and weather while sleeping is one of the biggest topics up for debate. No one wants to agree with anybody, and I know I'm probably going to get vicious hate mail for this entire chapter.

One thing we can all agree on, though, is that you need a sleeping bag.

CHOOSING A SLEEPING BAG

My standard sleeping setup for many years was a ridged-foam pad, a mummy sleeping bag, a liner, and my head, on the ground, wondering why my backpacking teachers, Chuck and Patchen, wouldn't let us have pillows.

The mummy sleeping bag is exactly as terrifying and uncomfortable as it sounds. It is essentially a puffy tube in the tapered shape of a sarcophagus. To get in, you lay it out flat, unzip it, slide yourself in, bend forward, zip it up as much as you can, lie back down, continue zipping it up, and then tug on the interior bungee cords until your shoulders are pinned to your body, like a straightjacket. You then shimmy your hands up your locked-down sides to insert your head into the bonnet attached to the top of the bag, and pull the bonnet's bungee straps down until your forehead has a friction burn and your lips, nose, and what remains of your eyes are the only things exposed to the soulless, frigid night. Then you sleep.

In Team, we used mummy bags in tandem with liners. Sleeping bag liners are basically bed condoms: thin polyester sheets sewn into the shape of a tube that you slip into before mummification. They prevent sleeping bags

from needing to be washed too often, which is handy, as washing a thin polyester sheet is much more efficient than washing a sleeping bag—in addition to being quite a cumbersome load of laundry, sleeping bags naturally lose a small amount of insulation with each wash. Liners add warmth, as well. After Team, I backpacked with an ancient, used sleeping bag for many years, never understanding why I was cold at night, no matter how much clothing I put on, when my backpacking partner wasn't. Finally, I bought a liner. The thin barrier of polyester between me and the cold fabric of the sleeping bag was a magic trick. I hated the extra step needed to get in and out of bed, but it's astounding how much warmth something so small and cheap can add. Consider getting one if you're working with a sleeping bag that has lost some of its fluff.

The thing that truly makes me hate mummy sleeping bags, though, despite their ubiquity, history, and warmth, is the debate you have with yourself once when you're inside one, and, suddenly, you have to pee. It takes forty-five minutes to get out of the bag, and then another sixty-two hours to get back into it. I will lie in my bag forever, arguing with myself over the pros and cons of reversing the mummification process, or trying

SLEEPING PADS

The other critical component of your sleep setup is your sleeping pad, a.k.a. your "backcountry mattress." Some people think these aren't worth bringing along. Those people are *really hardcore*. I am not *really hardcore*, so I bring one. It's not all about comfort, either; a sleeping pad provides extra warmth by lifting your body off the cold ground. Most sleeping pads are daringly slim and short, possibly not even long enough to get your whole body on. But even the extra-short ones keep your body temp up at night and prevent your already abused shoulders and hips from rubbing against the ground as you sleep.

Sleeping pads come in two categories: inflatable and foam. Foam pads, from a distance, look like the inside of an industrial heating vent, but made of spongey plastic. They tend to weigh a few ounces more than inflatable pads, but they are also cheaper and you don't have to worry about them springing any leaks. Inflatable pads, on the other hand, are like smooth blow-up surfboards, cut into the shape of a coffin. Inflatable pads pack down smaller and weigh less than foam pads, so naturally they cost much more. Sometimes they are proudly advertised as self-inflating, but this particular perk has always been lost on me. (It takes thirty minutes to self-inflate or three puffs of my breath. If I am lucky enough to have the lungs to backpack, I think I can handle the inconvenience of huffing into a valve for ten seconds.)

At any rate, inflatable pads are almost always the superior choice until, on the trail, you discover yours has a hole. It's always a microscopic hole, so you usually can't fix it until you go home and slather the whole thing in soapy water to see where the air is escaping. Once you've found the hole and patched it with a repair kit (or gaffer tape), you're usually fine, but it doesn't always help you on the trail. Despite this, I still backpack with an inflatable pad. They are so much more compact. (And also I stole my mom's a long time ago and I think she will have forgotten until she reads this book.)

to will myself to sleep with a full bladder. "But really? I mean you can just fall asleep, right? You don't need to get up and go. How bad could it be?" The argument always ends the same way: I have to get up and relieve myself. But still, you can spend up to two hours in a mummy sleeping bag, per night, thinking about your bladder.

This is why when someone told me about sleeping quilts, I was extremely intrigued. I was chatting with a woman who had hiked the entire PCT the year before, with a pack that weighed only thirteen pounds before food and water. Dutifully impressed, I asked her about her gear, and she was quite pleased to share her experience with a sleeping quilt, which I had never heard of.

"It's like a mummy sleeping bag, except without a zipper, so it splays out around you. Scientists discovered that you actually retain more heat this way. Sleeping in a mummy, which zips up around you, compresses half the down under your body weight, making it useless. The quilt drapes over you, so this doesn't happen."

"So scientists discovered blankets?" I said.

I was thrilled at the idea, though. The truth is I had been sleeping with my mummy unzipped over me like a quilt for a few years, because I simply couldn't handle the claustrophobia and the bathroom debates any longer. Now instead of feeling lazy, I feel scientifically vindicated, which is much nicer.

One last bit of advice on sleeping bags: You'll see them advertised in degree ratings like 32°F, 20°F, 0°F, etc. This means the bag is suitable for sleeping at that overnight temperature. I think this rating system is a little strange, as it can't possibly take into account whether your body runs hot or cold or what conditions you prefer to lull you to sleep. What a person clad in layers of long underwear and fleece wants out of a sleeping bag at 32°F might be very different from the needs of someone who forgot to pack pants, period. Still, manufacturers have to use some kind of classification. If you're going to buy one new, get the bag with the lowest rating you can find and afford. It's much easier to unzip a too-warm sleeping bag and let out body heat than to spend a night shivering in a lightweight sleeping bag with all your clothes on, blinking in the dark, wondering if you can some-how spoon your backpack for warmth since you don't have anything else to put on.

If you are still cold inside your sleeping bag with all your clothes on, and a pad raising your body off the ground, there is one last warm-up trick you can try that works weirdly well: eating.

Chapter 6

FOOD
Pop-Tarts Are Good
for You Now

"Of course you can take brie, everyone is just a p&*#%!"
—A backpacking expert

There are three schools of philosophy when it comes to backpacking food:

1. The purist: "My body is a temple, and on this most holy ground, I shall imbibe and masticate only the purest dehydrated vegetables, unsulfured fruits, and organic grains."
2. The lazy bear: "I don't really feel like portioning out olive oil or measuring dried chili into ziplock bags, so I'm going to buy twelve prepackaged freeze-dried meals and call it a day."
3. The opportunist: "Hail, Mary, full of grace, we're gonna have a trash party."

I, along with most people I know, am an opportunist. That's not to say there isn't merit to the other categories. I believe my body is a temple, and

I am sharply reminded of its value when it carries me into the wilderness. At home, I am a good girl who eats her greens, schedules her cardio, and would never eat fistfuls of Goldfish in bed (anymore). So why am I a category three eater when I backpack? Because the backcountry is that magical place where you can eat whatever you want, and still lose weight. I am not wasting that opportunity on kale.

For you category one eaters, there are entire books written about healthy backcountry cooking, dedicated to helping you craft meals that will no doubt keep your colon sparkling throughout your trip. If this matters greatly to you, go ahead and seek this advice out (you will not find much of it here from my muffiny self).

If you adhere to a special eating regime, such as veganism, gluten-free, or keto, it would be especially prudent to pick up a book that specializes in how to make your diet work in the backcountry. And it can work, I assure you. One good thing about the twenty-first century is that there is so much advice out there on how to stick to a particular eating pattern—even at 5,000 feet with nothing but an open flame and a single pot. I promise no matter how weird or imposing you think your diet is, there's a person out there with the same diet who has figured out meal ideas for backpacking. Don't let the fact that you can't eat things like noodles, nuts, or nature bars—the staples of the backcountry pantry—keep you from thinking you can backpack.

While you can and should stick to the same dietary restrictions you have at home, I do want to note that it's a pretty bad idea to think of your first backpacking trip as a good place to begin a weight-loss diet. Even if backpacking is part of some ultimate wellness journey for you, the backcountry is a terrible place to begin dieting.

Backpacking requires *fuckloads* of energy; you're in constant motion, and your back and legs are basically doing sixty-pound presses with every step. This is especially true if you're going uphill, but still applies on downhills and while walking across flat terrain. Your metabolism is about to become an inferno, burning double—sometimes triple—the calories you normally burn at home. The true planners among us actually do the math on this: I once met a guy who measured his basal metabolic rate, the distance he was walking, and elevation of his trip, among other factors, to ultimately determine he needed roughly 3,500 calories per day to maintain his body weight while walking. He all but force-fed himself to meet that intake, and when he came home after a week, he still clocked in ten pounds less than when he started. Fat loss is going to happen whether you like it or not. This is the time to consume all the calories you want. Rejoice, good people, and let us celebrate in the pasta aisle.

If you fancy yourself a modern nutritionist (i.e., you either have a degree in nutrition, or you have spent, like, a lot of time reading about carbs on Livestrong), you can take issue with me here. You can tell me that not all calories are created equal, certain foods will help or hurt your endurance and performance outside, and simple carbs are truly terrible for you.

I know. We all know. If you really are a nutritionist, you also probably know that this kind of all-day activity is the exact place where simple carbs finally have a chance to shine: your body will be grateful for the quick energy, as you'll be burning it almost as fast as you bring it in. You also know that your body will be sweating, so salt deserves a regular slot on the menu. Finally, there is the sad reality that it is essentially impossible to carry nutritious standards like fresh vegetables, ripe fruit, raw meat, or delicate things like eggs in your pack. The irony of Mother Nature's verdant, untamed backyard being the one place on earth where I regularly indulge in high-salt, preservative-laden, industrialized food products is not lost on me.

"But fiber! Don't you end up constipated and miserable?" You'd think, on an indefensible diet of white, dehydrated, factory-farmed grains with no fresh produce to speak of, this would be an issue. Come to think of it, I have no idea how I ever shit in the woods. There's basically zero fiber in my backpacking diet. Maybe there are prunes in my trail mix? I, too, am baffled.

Anyway, the point is, what's typically on a good backcountry menu is lightweight, calorically dense food that is easy to pack, doesn't need refrigeration, and can be prepared with little more than hot water. It's not my fault that mac 'n cheese, tuna preserved in a foil pouch, and hot cocoa powder happen to be in this category. What's not on the menu is anything squishy, refrigeration dependent, heavy, or bulky. Maybe you can treat yourself to fresh fruit or vegetables on your first night, but since everything in your pack is getting smashed pretty hard, by day three the consequences of bringing fresh foods can often be . . . ferment-y. I'm not saying this to scare you. I'm saying it to contextualize all the horrible things I'm about to tell you I do with dried potato flakes.

I know people who make extravagant meals out in the wilderness, flipping over their lids to griddle pancakes or magically turning their pots into ovens and baking biscuits. I have so much respect for these people. Mostly because I tried to bake once on a mountain in Chile, and instead of serving everyone fluffy, golden cinnamon rolls, I ended up scraping burned Bisquick batter off my friend's one-hundred-dollar titanium lid for an hour. Eventually, I had to give up and inform the party that every meal for the rest of the trip was going to be fill-in-the-blank with a side of charred cake.

The truth is, after hiking for eight hours, finding camp, setting up the tent, and facing the prospect of giving my quads and back a long rest, the last thing I want to do is cook. I want to eat.

PLANNING YOUR MEALS

Meal planning can run the gamut, depending on how much time, energy, and fuel you want to devote to eating out on the trail. Here are some common options for fast meals and easy snacks.

Breakfast

While backpacking, I invariably eat oatmeal for breakfast. I am a fan of the quick, just-add-water varieties. You can empty a packet or two into a pot of hot water, stir, and eat. At home I would probably eat just one of these for breakfast. In the backcountry I eat two, greedily. With my eyes shifting about in case any squirrels are getting ideas. Oatmeal is also very easy to clean up, as you can simply swish your pot with a bit of water and say, "OK, I did the dishes."

Sipping a hot drink while dewy leaves reflect the light of sunrise and birds flit to and fro heralding the day is one of the absolute brightest moments of backpacking. For this highly Instagramable event, I always bring along either instant coffee or instant tea. I used to brew only fresh tea leaves and coffee beans, but the purist romance of brewing myself a fresh cup of morning anything was soon eclipsed by my annoyance at having to pack out tea bags or guilt about chucking spent coffee grounds into the forest. If you're a coffee snob, you might find the idea of instant offensive, and that's OK. You can buy collapsible drippers and other compact tools that allow you to enjoy an artisanal pour over in the backcountry. But you really should pack out your grounds; remember all those LNT principles we talked about? Please don't be the jerk who thinks he can start a compost pile at every campsite.

While coffee is the traditional go-juice of most Western nations, there are a variety of teas, ideal for the kind of steady, long-term energy needed to climb mountains, that have been employed by non-Westerners for thousands of years. I am an especially big fan of yerba maté. It shares the same South American homeland as the coca plant, but without the annoyance of having everyone who sees you drinking it elbow you in the ribs and say, "Lol you know this is what they use to make cocaine." Yerba maté is the traditional drink of the Guaraní people whose legend tells that it was gifted to them by the goddess of the moon for longevity, vitality, and health. And I am not here to contradict a moon goddess.

The first time I had yerba maté was while hiking with Joanne and Irina. I was, hands down, the person in the worst shape. After lagging behind the pair of them for two days in a row, on the third morning, instead of coffee, I threw some maté leaves into my Nalgene. I sipped the tea throughout the morning, then when the liquid ran out, I started chewing on the leaves (traditional yerba maté prep involves sipping the tea through a straw with a strainer, to avoid the leaves getting in your mouth, but I didn't have that, so I just kinda went with the flow). By noon I was going off like an alarm clock. "Guys, are you OK? This really isn't that hard. C'mon, it's just a little farther. You guys should really try this tea. Hey, after this, do you want to build a house?"

Carbs are fuel. Caffeine is a performance-enhancing drug. Plan breakfast accordingly.

Lunch

My backcountry lunch is typically salami or tuna packs, paired with tortillas, cheese, and some kind of sauce. Salami is probably the biggest and heaviest indulgence I bring into the backcountry. I haven't checked with any historians, but I'm pretty sure jerky was the staple of questing heroes for thousands of years before energy bars were invented. By comparison, the cheese I bring is preposterously modern, and usually in stick form. "But don't those have to be refrigerated?" you ask. Read the label on your next pack of cheese sticks and ask me that question again. Normally I'd recommend you avoid anything containing propionic acid that advertises itself as edible, but damn if it doesn't stay clean and fresh through day four.

Once, while prepping for a trip to the Lost Coast in Northern California, and feeling osmotically hippieish and farm-to-table, Jeanne and I had the brilliant idea to put eight ounces of Dubliner Irish cheddar into my food pouch, thinking we could snack on it during lunches and toss a few cubes of gourmet into our otherwise humble mac 'n cheese at night. After three miles of walking on the beach, I took my pack off to grab some water and saw a strange stain on the nylon back. Tentatively, I touched it: my fingertip came back shiny. I opened up my pack and the rich scent of warm, fermented cow's milk punched me in the face. Then I pulled out our food pouch and found a golden blob of cheese, its life force leaking out all over the oatmeal, cocoa, tortillas, and protein bars.

That night, I dumped the entire cheese brick into a steaming pot of macaroni, looked a concerned Jeanne firmly in the eye, and stated, "This is not going back into my pack." It was the best thing we'd ever eaten. (But still probably a bad idea.)

I encourage you to have fun with your sandwich platter. Make a different one every day, and pack sauces that will go with different proteins and cheeses. To make whatever weird lunch sandwich I'm inventing a little more festive, I usually include some packets of mustard (grabbed from a fast-food restaurant or saved from Chinese takeout) to my food kit. These are lightweight, tidy, and do a lot to spice up a salami and cheese wrap. You can also buy tiny, refillable, silicone squeeze pouches, and fill them with all kinds of sauces, jams, and nut butters. Fill these with as much as you think you'll need for your trip, then wash them at home when it's over, and reuse them for many years. This is a great idea, so if you're not as cheap as I am, you should probably get some.

Snacks

Trail mix is in its natural habitat in the backcountry. It never goes bad, it contains a mix of proteins and good-for-you fats, and it's calorically dense as hell. The catch is that it's actually quite heavy, so I don't rely on it solely. I get enough for everyone to have one handful between breakfast and lunch each day, and another between lunch and dinner. Depending on the mix, and your hunger levels, you can even throw a scoop into your morning oatmeal, turning it into a multitextured, nutty granola (don't knock this until you try it).

Like trail mix, the protein bar was basically designed for people engaging in vigorous activity in the great outdoors. It's a hockey puck of protein and vitamins trying its darndest to taste like birthday cake. What's not to love? Find a brand you like and grab one for every day you'll be out.

Some ultraminimalists opt for protein powder at snack time, which is easy to shake up in your water bottle. Actually, some people do this for all three meals, to save weight and keep things simple. It makes sense, if you think about it, and while I applaud the efficiency, I'm pretty sure if I ate nothing but dehydrated vitamin dust for days on end, I'd be gnawing on tree bark by the end of my trip, just for variety.

Chocolate is a bad idea for snack time in the backcountry, for obvious, melty reasons. But gummy candies are safe. Jeanne and I took Swedish Fish on our very first trip after high school, our first venture without the protection of our teachers, or anyone but each other. Now I take Swedish Fish whenever I backpack, as a bit of a tradition. In fact, it has led to a Pavlovian condition where if I ever pop one into my mouth at home, I start smelling pine trees and my legs begin to cramp. Feel free to experiment for yourself.

Dinner

If I let a first date believe that what I eat for dinner while backpacking is what I eat at home, they'd get up, excuse themselves to go to the bathroom, and escape through the window.

Boxed mac 'n cheese is an easy, tasty, lightweight, calorically dense meal that can be enjoyed multiple times on a trip. But what comes in the box is just the beginning: you can make it interesting by throwing in a pouch of spiced tuna, a scoop of dehydrated chili, or even just some lemon pepper or a tiny pack of hot sauce pilfered from a Taco Bell.

Dehydrated foods, including soups, are a great idea—just be sure to add enough water.[27] Almost all grains and beans come in an "instant" form, sometimes called "dehydrated" or "microwaveable," that requires little more than a splash of hot water and three minutes of patience to turn into a functioning meal. The instant versions of these grains aren't as pure as their parents, to be sure, but they require so much less fuel. You'll be tired at the end of the day, so I encourage you to give yourself the gift of not waiting forty-five minutes for dinner, and, more importantly, not having to carry the fuel it takes to cook a forty-five-minute dinner.

Rice, lentils, quinoa, and couscous can be enlivened by mixing in beans and/or dehydrated veggies. You can even throw in some salami for a proper stew, and season with spices. (I'm a fan of blends—something you've worked with at home that you know will dependably improve nearly anything you throw it on.) Pill carriers work particularly great for backcountry spice storage.

If I'm being brutally honest, though, I rarely bring spices on backpacking trips. I keep telling myself I'm going to start cooking interesting, healthy backcountry meals that will make me the envy of my outdoor peers—in fact, I own several books on this topic. But on the trail, I invariably end up eating three things: mac 'n cheese, mashed potatoes, and stuffing (usually not at the same time . . . usually). It's just too easy, especially the mashed potatoes and stuffing. You basically just throw the powdery contents of each pack into hot water, wait ten minutes, open the lid, and boom: you have a Thanksgiving dinner to pair with your sunset. It is becoming of a king.

"What about butter or margarine?" you ask. "Don't a lot of boxed meals require one of those?" Sort of. Listen, the real secret to backcountry cooking is that backpacking makes food taste better, even when you make it wrong. This doesn't make you tasteless. When I was twenty-two, I visited a small, upscale, organic winery in Napa with my older sister, who was (and is) extremely fucking cool and classy and very into doing things like

---

27. What moisture a dehydrated food doesn't take from the pot, it will take from your body. Since you will likely be running low on fluids at the end of the day, don't be afraid to overdo it when you "just add water."

educating her younger sister about the different tertiary aromas between an old vine Zin and an expressive Cab. We sampled a sip from a seventy-dollar bottle of organic, garnet liquid, and I was one of the few people at the table who could actually detect the "Rutherford dust" known to be delicately lingering on the back palette. My sister smiled. I flushed with pride.

So when I tell you I've stolen shelf-stable miniature tubs of butter and brought them into the backcountry in order to make a box of Rice-A-Roni exactly as directed, and that, on a different trip, I couldn't tell the difference in taste when I forgot the butter, don't accuse me of being a Philistine. There's enough salt and spice in most boxed meals to preserve them through the millennium. You can definitely get away with not bringing butter into the backcountry. Just keep a little bit more water in the pot than what the directions call for, so things will still stir nicely. Alternately, you can carry a little squeeze bottle of olive oil. You might taste the difference, but my "Rutherford dust" tongue cannot.

PACKING YOUR FOOD

There's a delicate balance to strike when packing meals for the backcountry. On the one hand, you don't want to take too much food because you'll be carrying a ton of unnecessary weight. On the other hand, you don't want to take too little because then you'll be miserable and hungry. You'll be my fellow Team classmate Florence, huddled against a rock in Joshua Tree National Park, slowly reaching a thin arm toward another person in her party and asking, "Can you pass the candied pecans?" Because she's starving, and all they brought for snacks were a few expensive handfuls of what your grandmother serves at Sunday bridge club to impress her neighbors.

The best way to ensure you're packing enough, but not too much, is to pre-portion your meals out for every single day. Sort of like someone on a diet—a diet that magically insists you eat freeze-dried fettucine Alfredo and instant potatoes. The way my first backpacking teachers taught me to do this was to put every meal in its own ziplock bag and label it: breakfast one, lunch one, dinner four, etc. There might be a few things that traverse days, like spices, coffee, or a bulk bag of dehydrated soup meant to be part of multiple dinners, but you get the idea. As you put each meal into a dedicated ziplock, remove as much packaging as possible. Mac 'n cheese? Kill

the box, and pour the noodles and the cheese packet right into the baggy. Tub of hot cocoa? Take a few scoops and put them directly in their own baggy. Removing excess packaging reduces the presence of any dreaded "empty" space in your pack, and also lowers the amount of trash you'll have to pack out. If you have any particularly persnickety dinners that require explicit measurements, you can always write down instructions on a scrap of paper and pop them in the baggy too.

I realize this level of organization might seem like overkill—it was designed for teenagers who, if left to their own devices, might pack nothing but a few boxes of gushers and Slim Jims (or candied pecans) for a week in the wilderness. But it really is an excellent way to make sure you're packing the Goldilocks amount of food: enough to ensure you'll be well-fed, but not so much that you're carrying unnecessary weight. Food can easily become the heaviest item in your pack, and the effort in prep now is worth the physical effort you'll save on the trail.

Once you're done packing up your meals, throw them all into a dry sack, the backpacker's magical "bag of holding," to keep them separate from your other gear. This precaution is mostly in case something bursts to keep you from having to clean cheese powder from the crevices of your backpack for the next seven months. You'll find it's pretty easy to fit your food bag in your backpack, often with room to spare. But before you consider yourself done, double-check whether your food bag will need to fit into a bear canister at night.

Bear canisters aren't just for food. Any and all scented items, including sunscreen, bug spray, and lip balm, have to go into this container at the end of the day. It's both for your protection, and the bear's. A bear doesn't really know the difference between a thin mint and a tube of toothpaste, and probably won't care about your attempts to explain it in the moment.

The alternative to the bear canister is a "bear bag," a technique that involves tying your food sack to a rope, tying the other end of the rope to a stuff sack filled with small rocks, and engaging in a wild game of flinging. I have done this once, out of desperation, because my backpacking party forgot to test if all our food and scented items could fit inside the bear canister before we left the house. Seeing who could get the winning shot

THE INFAMOUS BEAR CANISTER

Bear canisters are the credit scores of the backpacking world: they're required to visit most of America's most popular backpacking zones, while at the same time being a complete racket. They are essentially eighty-dollar plastic buckets with locking lids, and they only come in two sizes: clutch purse and airplane hangar. Many ultralighters resent the space they take up in their pack, and cheapskates gnash their teeth at the cost. Two companies make them, and I'm disappointed that I'm not in one of their CEO's wills.

Despite the fact that they are made from a kind of plastic that isn't going to decompose until the year 3000, they are difficult to find used. However, if the park or forest you're visiting requires backpackers to use bear canisters (this will be made abundantly clear when you are looking up your route), oftentimes you can rent one for a measly few bucks. You just have to get to the ranger station when they're open—I have never found this feasible, because I invariably arrive at a park's entrance gate in the middle of the night after getting off work at five o'clock and then driving four hours. But still, it's a great program.

was a fun midafternoon sport. Rangers increasingly frown upon hanging a bear bag, in light of the repeated evidence that bears are frighteningly intelligent creatures, and generally better at climbing trees than humans are. Exceptions exist in certain national parks, where land managers still provide poles, wires, or similar systems to help you hang your food. In some other parks, a bear canister is mandatory, and you can be fined if you are caught storing food without one. As you plan your trip, check with the managing agency to find out whether they require a canister.

Bear country makes up a large portion of the American National Park System (including parts of the Sierra, the Rockies, the Appalachians, and, I think, the entire state of Alaska, where bears actually drive trucks, attend church functions, and participate in their local 4-H club).

The good news is that bear canisters serve multiple functions beyond deterring bears. They protect your food and scented items from all manner of nibbling forest critters. As you eat your meals and your canister empties over the course of your trip, you can store your stove or other small items in there to make use of the empty space. It can even double as a wash basin or a little chair.[28]

TURNING POWDER INTO DINNER

I pine for a time I have never lived in, when cowboys could ride into the middle of nowhere, stop anywhere they liked, gather whatever wood they found, cook a can of pork 'n beans over an open fire, then toss the empty can into a bush, and drift off to sleep to the crackling lullaby of the logs. Everything I just described is currently illegal in California.

If your dream backpacking trip involves a cheerful campfire under the stars to warm your hands and cook your meals, you'll first have to find a location that still allows people to have fires in the backcountry. Both state and national parks across the country restrict wilderness campfires, either by banning them outright or by enforcing lengthy rules at various elevations, seasons, and locations. Frequently in the summer there are all-out bans. National forests and BLM lands may have fewer restrictions, but you can still run into a lot of red tape there too.

When you're getting your permit, rangers usually let you know in no uncertain terms whether you can have an open campfire outside of a developed fire ring—and the answer (at least in California) is generally "hell no." This isn't something to sneeze at—many wildfires have been started by well-meaning campers and hikers. Building a campfire in the wilderness during the dry season, miles away from any firefighting teams, is like playing with matches next to kerosene. Even if you don't agree with the spirit of the rule, it's not like fires are particularly sneaky. Entire cultures use smoke as a form of long-distance communication. It will not be hard for rangers to find you and fine you, if they want to.

Considering how unlikely they are to be legal, I'm not going to spend a lot of time here telling you how to ethically build a campfire in the backcountry (such as, being sure to look for an already used ring, how to dig a trench around the firepit, whether or not to stack rocks, and the importance

---

28. Never, ever, ever, ever sit on a bear canister if you aren't 100 percent certain the lid is completely and fully closed, unless you are in possession of Thor's hammer, because if you do, that's what you will need to get it open again.

FIRESTARTERS

I've noticed that, when starting a fire, a lot of people like to get fancy and bust out the Swiss magnesium wunderstriker that sheds indestructible sparks, or extra-long matches that burn brightly even when plunged underwater. While these are impressive marvels of human engineering, and they'll no doubt get the job done, I'd encourage you to ignore them in favor of the plastic lighters currently on display by the Ho Hos at your local gas station.

They weigh less than a feather and one, even the smallest size, should last for weeks. They light when it's wet out; they light when it's freezing. Scientists and YouTubers are online right now, ready and waiting to show you their research on this. These things could light on the surface of Pluto, I swear. The disposable lighter is the closest thing to a perfect tool man has ever created. And they're available everywhere, for a dollar. Throw a couple in your stove kit—I promise, they're all the firestarter you'll ever need.

of completely drowning the fire before you go to bed). There are tons of books on *How to Be a Completely Self-Sufficient He-Man Lumbergod in the Woods* that already cover this topic in clinical detail, so I'll leave that to those authors.

Instead, I'd like to focus on the reality of how you're going to cook your food while backpacking, which is with a stove. You'll need one that will work in all environments—whether you're above the tree line, in the rain, in the snow—along with a few tiny pieces of kitchen equipment.

Stoves

Stoves are like backpacks: there's so many of them out there, at so many different price points and with so many conflicting reviews, that it can be frustrating to figure out where to spend your money. On the cheaper end, there are alcohol stoves, which you can easily build at home from a tuna can. In the midrange are little $50 butterfly-looking thingamajiggies that attach directly to fuel canisters (usually isobutane) and spit out a single flame that's adjustable between "matchstick" and "flamethrower." Then you have $200 flameless, radiant-heat stoves that are essentially portable volcanos, lighting up a disc of magma under your pot and boiling water in two minutes. In the snow.

I had a miserable time finding a backpacking stove I liked. Granted, you have to practice a certain amount of radical acceptance if your goal is to boil water in the middle of nowhere in ten minutes or less with nearly no wood. From a historical perspective, this is basically a miracle, so it's best to lower your expectations now, especially if you're not planning on spending a lot of money.

The standard when I was taking my first trips was the MSR Whisperlite, a compact butterfly stove made of folded metal wings and tubes. It used white gas, which I kept in a fire-department-red refillable gas canister about the size of a bicycle water bottle. To ensure the gas flowed correctly, you had to first pressurize the canister with a specialized pump top. There was a very specific order in which you had to pump, plug in the fuel cable to the metal butterfly, and then actually put a light to the thing. I don't remember what it is, because all I remember about that time of my life is that I hated the MSR Whisperlite, and one of my life goals was to never have to use one ever again. Despite their reputation for reliability, things seem to go wrong with them easily and quickly in my experience.

When I visited Torres del Paine, there were so many people in the park that the rangers mandated we all cook in what was more or less a grange with a lot of open windows. We were told not to worry about fumes, despite the eager and frequent warning labels on our cooking equipment that said "never under any circumstances use me inside." We listened to the people who could fine us, rather than the inanimate stickers.

A Russian couple sat down across from me inside the crowded grange, and I watched intently as one of them pulled out an MSR Whisperlite. He methodically and cautiously pumped the top of the gas canister until liquid fuel squirted into the stove pan. I saw in his eyes that, while he wasn't certain, he was pretty sure this was part of the process. I said nothing and decided I, too, thought it was part of the process, despite a small, nagging feeling in the back of my mind that said "you should move away from this situation." And so when, a few moments later, the whole system erupted in

Choose your stove carefully and practice before your trip. Left to right: A chimney stove, a refillable white gas stove, a compressed canister stove, and an integrated insulated stove system

happy yellow flames dancing far beyond his cookpot and up to the ceiling, we were all a bit taken aback.

Flash forward to a few years later, the morning before Jeanne and I dragged our partners into the arid, sulfuric mysteries of Northern California's Lassen Volcanic National Park on their first-ever backpacking trips. Jeanne was pacing over crunchy rocks and biting her nails in quiet frustration under a pine tree, because she hadn't had her coffee yet, because the Whisperlite wouldn't work. Despite her numerous cleanings, reorientings, and prayers to pagan gods, it ended up taking her husband, a trilingual physicist with a PhD, one hour of meticulously unscrewing and rescrewing every piece to finally get a flame out of it. (I think it's possible that the express promise of "field repairs" is the reason the Whisperlite is so popular among the Boy Scout set of backpackers.)

My current stove isn't much better, though. It is a Solo Stove, a type of "chimney stove" that uses wood and sticks as fuel, and maximizes burn efficiency with an internal wall and specially engineered holes to guide smoke and air. It is basically a Bushbuddy, the original chimney stove popular in the early 2000s, that has somehow figured out how to get around copyright infringement.

The selling point, for me, was the promise of a stove that used nothing but forest detritus as fuel. So many stoves require the use of a special gas, or a special fuel canister, whether it's MSR, Jetboil, or another system. I was tired of these systems, tired of trying to do the math to figure out how much fuel I needed to carry, tired of lugging around used-up, uncrushable canisters that took up space in my backpack, tired of watching mishaps with fuel lines, spillage, clogged joints, and every other snag you might reasonably expect from a delicate engineering bauble in the uncontrolled environment that is wilderness. I loved the idea of not having to deal with any of that. The marketing for the Solo Stove told me I could simply gather small handfuls of the twigs and leaves that Mother Nature had left on the ground, and that would be all the fuel I would ever need. The manufacturer recommends "hard, dry twigs," but insists anything on the forest floor will work just fine.

The things we believe from Kickstarter videos. Cut to me, with a fistful of leaves and twigs, sitting in a campground near Mount Rainier National Park in Washington State, in direct sight line of a new boyfriend and all his friends, on my twentieth minute of trying to get a pot of water to boil over an adorable little chimney dutifully pumping out nothing but soot.

Over the course of these twenty minutes, the fire had alternated between candlewick and billowing flames, but the water never seemed to break past "kinda hot." Also during these twenty minutes, I learned that hard twigs burn longer and better than leaves and soft sticks. I learned that leaves produce more smoke than fire. I learned my pot was too big for the fire the stove was able to produce. In fact, I learned a lot of things anyone who has ever taken a basic course in outdoor fire building probably learns, just very quickly and in front of a boy I was trying to impress. Finally, after a full internal debate about all my life choices, I gave up on the water ever boiling, doused the fire angrily, and spent the rest of the day figuring out how to get soot off the bottom of an aluminum pot while you're camping. (Spoiler: You don't. Some people online suggest you pre-treat your pot with a bar of soap, but I don't carry bars of soap with me while backpacking, because no one does that.)

After the trip—feeling crushed, incompetent, and altogether a bit of a nincompoop—I still didn't want to let go of the dream the Solo Stove had sold me. However, it began to dawn on me how impractical depending on a specific kind of twig for fuel actually was. What if I wanted to use the stove above tree line? In the rain? Although our conception of "the great outdoors" usually involves an image of a forest, there are so many circumstances in the wilderness where you're not in a forest at all, and dry, hard twigs are not actually available. I realized the incredible prudence of synthetic fuel, and why, despite the trappings of anti-industrialism and self-sufficiency the backpacking world surrounds itself with, it has become ubiquitous.

So, swallowing my pride and letting go of my dream of being a spring dryad capable of creating flame with nothing more than a few snappy twigs and a puff of sweet breath, I bought the Solo Stove's alcohol burner, advertised as an "add-on" to the Solo Stove's chimney system. In reality though, the alcohol burner is its own stove: a dish the size of a tuna can that you fill with denatured alcohol, set alight, and then cook upon. It has little air holes encircling the top and a lid that controls the size of the flame. While standalone alcohol stoves are manufactured by many companies (perhaps most famously, Trangia), in fact, you can make one yourself out of an actual tuna can (or a soda can, or a cat food can)—there are a million blogs and YouTubers that can show you how.[29] But after the whole experience at Mount Rainier, I was not feeling particularly confident in my DIY crafting skills, so I shelled out the money for a professionally manufactured one, and experimented with it in my apartment's parking lot back home.

Lighting an alcohol stove is truly too easy. You fill the tin with ethanol, and, if you're pairing it with a chimney like I did, drop it into the center chamber. Then, with great care and sudden appreciation for your arm hair and eyebrows, lower a flame down into it. The alcohol lights instantaneously. The "amazing" chimney is little more than a windscreen and pot balancer at this point, but that is still quite useful. Some people (mostly ultralighters) have found they can use an alcohol stove without a windscreen or anything else to help balance or protect the flame under the pot. I can't recommend this, though; in fact, in many wilderness areas in California, standalone alcohol stoves go through phases of being banned altogether. Sometimes, oddly, these restrictions aren't super clear or openly communicated by the managing agency. All I know

---

29. Andrew Skurka, Homemade Wanderlust, and Mountains with Megan to name a few.

is that I have lived through four California wildfire seasons, and the idea of knocking over a bright ball of waterproof fire in the forest makes me feel faint. I don't need a park ranger to tell me this is risky. For this reason, I rarely use the alcohol stove anymore, and have returned to the tribe of the butterfly stove and fuel canister. Modern incarnations of butterfly stoves are compact, foolproof, alarmingly affordable, and emit strong, efficient heat. Above all, using one makes me feel like a better steward of the land.

No matter what you do, your stove system will have its quirks. You should make it a point to test out whichever one you pick before you head into the backcountry. Know what it likes, what it doesn't like, how it takes its coffee, and whether it enjoys long walks on the beach. In fact, take it for a long walk on the beach, or another day hike, and practice there first.

I'm still not a pure, self-sufficient mountain woman or serene, attuned-with-nature dryad, but at least I can make water boil in the rain.

Other Kitchen Equipment

My browser cookies, working diligently, frequently serve me advertisements for multistory, smartly stackable backcountry cutlery and cook sets. They look really nice, if sort of like a bad game of Jenga waiting to happen.

The kitchen is where my minimalism (or laziness, if we're being less charitable) really shows in the backcountry. Once you realize you can pull off a successful trip with one lidded pot, two sporks, and a pocketknife, it's really hard to let anyone convince you to take anything else. One time I even forgot the sporks (my partner whittled chopsticks out of some willing sticks). Frankly, you don't even need a mug if you bring at least one hard-sided water bottle—it's very pleasant to begin a morning with a Nalgene full of tea, warming your hands as well as your insides.

"But what about plates?" I can hear some formalists worry. "What are you supposed to eat off of?" If there are only two of you, just pass the pot of whatever yummy meal you made back and forth. (Don't scoff—I'm a sharer. What kindergarten did you go to?) If there are three of you, two of you can share the pot, and the other person can eat off the pot lid. I can't tell you how much space and weight a good sharing attitude will save.

But, if you find my manners atrocious, there are other options. I have a friend who took bone china plates—a wedding gift—on a honeymoon backpacking trip with her husband. It didn't occur to the love-besotted newlyweds that these fragile, heirloom objects might be poorly suited to a landscape of perilous cliffs and jagged rocks. The best part about this story is that it worked. They ate off of china plates for an entire week in the Himalayas—in the wind, in the rain—and they didn't break. So you can take my advice, and share a pot with your friends. You can grab a few containers out of your Tupperware drawer. Or you can bring wedding china. Choose your own adventure.

The thing to not cheap out on, however, is your cutlery. One time, before a backcountry excursion to Crater Lake, Oregon, I thought I was the cleverest fox in the den for not buying a fifteen-dollar titanium spork, and instead pocketing some take-out forks from a Taco Bell off the I-5. Plastic is just plastic, right?

Turns out, no. The plastic forks you get with your drive-thru carnitas fries aren't up for the task of working in scalding water. Six miles from the trailhead, I plunged my fork into a simmering pot, began to stir, then realized I wasn't cooking anymore so much as fighting a losing battle against a pot of macaroni. You don't need a different utensil for every step in the cooking process; you can use the same one to prep, stir, mash, and eat. Just make sure it's heat-resistant plastic, silicone, or metal designed for boiling temperatures.

Next to the utensils at your outdoor retailer of choice are a wide variety of cooking pots to choose from. Generally speaking, a one-liter pot will serve two to three people. Titanium is the gold standard (no wordplay intended), as it is incredibly lightweight and nearly impossible to bend or dent. However, an aluminum pot works just as well in my experience. If money is tight, don't be afraid to buy a used pot—just try to avoid steel, iron, or ceramics, as they'll likely be too heavy.

A final factor to consider is whether the size of your pot matches the size of your stove: powerful radiant-heat stoves can bring two-to-three-liter pots to a boil, but a little tin alcohol stove won't be able to heat much past a liter. Whatever pot you get, be sure it has a lid. In the backcountry, a lid is not just something you put over boiling water. It is a plate, a leftover saver, a cutting board, a mirror, and a Frisbee. What a sidekick.

CLEANING UP

During our high school backpacking program, I, along with most of my classmates, quickly realized the futility of washing dishes in the backcountry. We practiced Leave No Trace, as everyone should, which meant running to the edge of a lake, filling up a clean pot with water, carrying it at least two hundred feet away from the shore, squirting some soap into it, washing and scraping all our mugs and pots and bowls, then getting up to carry more fresh water with a different pot from the lake to rinse everything. The whole process involved a lot of walking, and it took about twenty minutes. We had been walking all day. We were tired. This was lame.

One by one we kind of gave up on the idea of making our dishes sparkle. Meals began to invariably end with someone simply pouring clean water into the cook pot, giving it some vigorous swishes, walking a bit away from camp, dumping out the pot, and calling it a day. Thus, we established what became known as the "obvious bits rule," coined by my compatriot Lauren. You could call the dishes done as long as you had removed all the obvious bits (i.e., you wouldn't have any *obvious* bits of black bean soup floating in your breakfast oatmeal, or any breakfast oatmeal stowing away in your evening couscous). The obvious bits rule works best if you're making simple meals that don't involve much added oil or burned bits stuck to the bottom of the pot, which is part of why I like to keep my meals so simple.

I've been trying to make "the obvious bits" official backpacking slang for years, because I know loads of backpackers follow this rule, even if they haven't named it like we did. If you think this is gross, and prefer a tidier kitchen, there are portable, lightweight backcountry "sinks" that fold up neatly and allow you to carry large volumes of water from a lake over to your camp to do your dishes properly.

But, it turns out, I'm not just a lazy teenager—I'm a lazy adult too. So I continue to practice the rule of obvious bits.

Chapter 7

WATER
A.K.A. "Poison Control"

"Gee-arr-diya, Gee-arr-diya / You're gonna get / Gee-arr-diya"
  —My roommate

When I was a little kid, my mom would sometimes take me along to run errands. One day, we were walking in an outdoor strip mall, on our way to get some potting soil. The mall had a little creek running nearby, a thin stream babbling under a decorative bridge. She pointed at the water.

"If you're ever in the backcountry, never, ever drink water without treating it," said my mother. "But if you have to, only if you really have to, make sure you drink from where it's running fastest. See how it rushes over those rocks? There will be less debris. It's as clean as you'll get it."

I nodded dutifully. We continued on to the nursery.

Ten years later, I was in the kitchen, chopping up a bell pepper. My mother walked in and opened the cupboard. She nibbled thoughtfully on a handful of crackers.

"When you go into the wild, the first thing you need to do is find your water," she said. "Everybody thinks it's shelter first, but water is the most important thing. Find water, then make shelter, then find food. That's the order of operations."

I again nodded dutifully, and filed this away in case I was ever hopelessly lost in the middle of nowhere, rather than making stir-fry on a Tuesday afternoon in the suburbs.

My mother was not wrong. Water is critical. You can go for quite a while without food, even if it's unpleasant, but without water your health meter runs out much faster.

One of my backpacking teachers, Chuck, diligently taught all his high school students that a liter an hour is the rule of thumb for staying hydrated in the backcountry. When we groaned at the weight of the water he made us carry, he simply said, "Well then, drink up. It's better in you than on you." He told us that if our urine wasn't clear, we should drink more water. If we felt thirsty, it meant we were already dehydrated, and should drink

PICKING OUT A WATER BOTTLE

Most backpackers opt to carry at least three liters of water on their person at all times. In places with a lot of stream crossings, you can reduce this, but in places where you will maybe hit only one water source a day, you might actually want to carry six or more. This is especially true if you aren't camping near water. What's the most efficient vessel for transporting this much liquid bounty? Let's explore some options.

» **Military Canteen:** The iconic image of a person lost in the desert usually includes one of these slung over their shoulder, its metallic base reflecting a wink of sunlight through a break in its canvas dressing. The bearer will occasionally lift it to the sky, tilt the bottom side toward heaven, and shake any remaining drops onto their chapped lips, while heat waves wiggle in the air. I don't know anyone who carries these in the backcountry, especially the desert. I also don't know why the military thought it was a good idea to make a water bottle out of something as heavy as metal, and then, for good measure, put it in a dress. But I've never sieged Guatemala's democratically elected government, so what do I know.

» **Nalgene:** An indestructible plastic tube that fits nicely in your hand, Nalgenes have a wide mouth for easy refills and side measurement marks to help in the backcountry kitchen. These features made it all but standard issue for backpackers in the last few decades of the twentieth century. Then, in the early 2000s, a scandal involving BPA leaching from plastic put them out of fashion in favor of newer steel and aluminum bottles. But many die-hard fans would not give them up. The company released a BPA-free version in 2008, which is what you see on store shelves today.

» **Metal Flasks:** Modern, metal-based water bottles like Klean Kanteen and Hydro Flask surged in popularity after the dangers of BPA were discovered. They may dent if dropped, burn your hands when filled with hot liquid, and weigh a touch more than Nalgenes, but a lot of people prefer to use them rather than keep up on the research about which petrochemical in your gear has now been proven to invert your gonads or make your chin grow eyes.

» **Disposable Water Bottle:** Yep, the kind you get at a gas station for ninety-nine cents with water already in it. According to most companies that produce these bottles, they are not supposed to be reused (mostly because of all the chemicals that leach from the plastic into the water). The narrow mouth can also make them hard to refill. However, many backpackers find disposable water bottles light, ample, and durable enough for several weeks on the trail. For ease of use, this bottle scores a ten.

» **Bladder:** Soft, multi-liter, plastic pouches. Imagine the head of a deflated octopus with a long straw sticking out of it. The most famous bladder is probably the Platypus, which many bikers, hikers, and rock climbers swear by. Your backpack may even have a slim, designated pouch where the bladder can sit as you hike. They are large, easy to fill, squeeze into any space, and reduce in size as they empty. You have to get over the concept of sipping from something called a "bladder" using a warm, flaccid straw, but after that, wow, what a device.

» **Collapsible Water Reservoir:** Stiff plastic bags that, when empty, roll up like used tubes of toothpaste. As with disposable water bottles, the narrow mouth can be hard to fill, but if you're into saving space or know that you have a few days where you'd rather be carrying seven liters than three, this option can't be beat.

more water. If we were tired, we should drink more water. If we were getting mauled to death by a rabid skunk, we should drink more water. We assumed he was drinking water even while urinating—Nalgene in one hand and stream guided by the other, like a cherub in a water fountain.

Some people find drinking a liter of water an hour far too difficult. I do not. I am a naturally thirsty person; I am in constant possession of a water bottle, and I panic when it's empty. I have never once in my life been told to drink water, because I'm usually pushing other people out of the way to get to the sink. Sometimes I wonder if I have a glandular disorder or something.

I have hiked with those who aren't like this, however. I've watched them balk at the idea of having to drink so much, and then kind of forget to put life juice in their mouths on the trail, quickly falling into cranky moods and exhaustion. Regardless of whether you're like me or find the idea of drinking a liter of water an hour scandalous, I would encourage you to pay a little more attention than normal to how much water you are drinking while backpacking. Consider water lubrication for your body, which is walking all day. Not drinking enough is obviously dangerous in hot weather (leading to heat exhaustion and heat stroke), but it's deceptively dangerous in cold weather too. Every time you drop your pack, stop to take a picture, or scream at your partner for getting you lost, it's a good idea to have a swig.

I am aware that, with this advice, there is a risk of overhydration—when you consume so much water you lower your sodium levels and develop hyponatremia—but that condition is so incredibly rare I hesitate to even mention it. You are far more likely to underhydrate than overhydrate while backpacking. No matter where or in what temperature you're hiking, your muscles need a lot more water to move and carry all this stuff on your back than they need at home. Backpacking frequently involves sweating through your clothes, climbing uphill in hot weather, or nursing a sunburn. You can lose up to two to three liters of water an hour in those conditions. To keep up, you honestly might have to consume an amount you would find comical at home (such as a liter an hour).

HOW TO DRINK THE WATER YOU FIND

One of the saddest things about backpacking is that no matter how clean the water looks, you probably can't drink it. This is the reality of living on

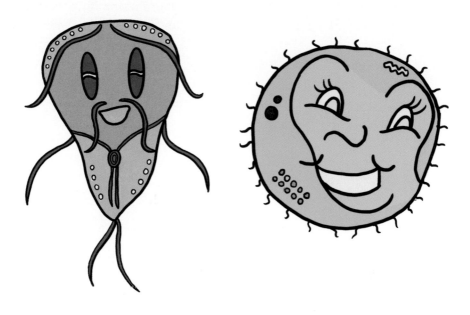

Waterborne villains

earth in the twenty-first century. Even deep in the wilderness, tiny dregs of civilization are there to ruin your good time.

Specific waterborne villains vary by region (heavy metals and E. coli are bigger concerns on the East Coast), but cryptosporidium and giardia are the two main bugs to worry about in the United States. Cryptosporidium (lovingly nicknamed "crypto" before Bitcoin was invented) is a parasite. It looks like a balloon filled with hot dogs under a microscope, and its only dream in life is to have a police riot in your small intestine for a few weeks. Giardia is also a parasite, but it looks kind of like a lamprey had a love child with a tuba. It wants to throw a birthday party in your pants.

They won't kill you or even mangle you (usually). More often, these parasites will sit in your gut throughout your entire trip, and then strike when you're at home, calm and secure that everything went off without a hitch. The symptoms generally manifest as a terrifically bad bout of stomach flu (one that may or may not land you in the ER), but they usually pass with time and maybe a little medication.

However, you don't need to worry about giardia or crypto at all, because you're not going to get them. You're going to clean your water before you drink it. There are three ways to do this: boil it, treat it with chemicals, or use a water filter or purifier.

Boiling

Boiling is the fail-safe, the universal truth for creating drinkable water. Put your water in a pot, light your stove, give it a few minutes at a rolling boil, let it cool, and then drink up. But this should be your backup plan, since boiling all your water would take an insane amount of time and fuel. This is why most backpackers prefer to use chemicals or filters.

Chemicals

When I first started backpacking in Team, we purified all our water with an iodine solution called Polar Pure. It was a two-inch-tall glass vial of water with iodine pellets trapped at the bottom. The iodine pellets leached into the water in the vial, ultimately creating a concentrated solution of liquid iodine that you could then add to your water bottle in the backcountry, killing anything you picked up every time you dipped it into a river or stream. When the vial was empty, you just added more water, shook it up with the pellets, waited a few hours, and then were good to go again. It was lightweight, never expired, required no batteries or manual labor, worked in any temperature, and generally promised to carry you, safely hydrated, from here to the zombie apocalypse.

Many years later, I tried to buy my own Polar Pure, and couldn't find it anywhere. Aquamira makes a tablet form of iodine, but as I've been trying to buy backpacking supplies that can reasonably moonlight as end-of-the-world supplies, I really had my heart set on the bottle of refillable Polar Pure. I found out it had been pulled from the market because people were using it to make meth. (I ended up buying some on eBay, probably from someone making meth.)

The downside of iodine is it makes your water taste like . . . well . . . iodine. To compensate for the taste, in Team, we would sprinkle flavored vitamin C packets or powdered Gatorade into our water. It helped more than you might think, but it was still pretty nasty. Taking iodine orally for more than two weeks is also not recommended, as it can affect your thyroid.[30]

Anyway, back in 2005, I was taught that iodine killed everything. But that was back when the only contaminant anyone in the backpacking community was really talking about was giardia. Then crypto became the new famous bad guy after infecting a few water treatment plants in the Midwest, and scientists discovered that iodine doesn't actually kill it.

Chlorine dioxide tablets, on the other hand, supposedly kill all parasites, bacteria, and viruses if you toss them into your water and wait about four hours—at least according to the people who make them.[31] What you do during those four hours while you wait to drink your water is up to you, I guess.

Water Filters and Purifiers

Water filters are actually different from water purifiers, even though most people use these terms interchangeably (I did, at least, before I learned the difference). In backpacking, a water *filter* strains out parasites and bacteria, whereas a water *purifier* strains, kills, or otherwise eliminates both those pathogens, plus viruses. In the United States, a filter is generally fine, but if you're traveling elsewhere, especially places where Hepatitis A is known to hang out, you should consider either buying a purifier, or pairing a filter with a chemical purifier like iodine or chlorine dioxide.

I had a really nice pump water filter once. A gift from my brother-in-law, it was my most prized backpacking possession and was far fancier than anything I could have afforded on my own at the time. It got stolen out of my bag on an Aeroméxico flight on my way home from Patagonia (they refused to acknowledge the theft or replace the filter). My hope is that at least someone else's drinking water is clean now.

---

30. I guzzled this stuff for years. Huh, maybe I do have a glandular problem.

31. Potable Aqua, for example, makes two kinds of chlorine water treatment tablets: chlorine dioxide and sodium dichloroisocyanurate. According to the Centers for Disease Control and Prevention, chlorine dioxide is the only type of chlorine that can kill crypto. But they go on to note that chlorine dioxide has only "a low to moderate effectiveness in killing Cryptosporidium." Meanwhile, the manufacturers of chlorine dioxide water purification tablets simply say they are "effective." How reassuring for us all.

Meet your defense force: a gravity filter, pump filter, UV purifier, and squeeze filter

Bitter about this experience, I refused to buy another pump filter and instead purchased a squeeze-bag system. To use a squeeze filter, you scoop untreated water into a bag, screw a little nozzle doohickey onto the top, and then squeeze the bag's contents through the nozzle (which contains the filter) and into your water bottle. The whole process takes about five minutes for a few liters of water. I found this to be a welcome respite from the pump filter, which, despite its lofty reputation, took forever and had so many tubes and hoses flopping about rudely that it became remarkably difficult to keep them from contaminating each other. Even with a squeeze bag, you'll still find yourself doing yogic goddess squats at the edge of a creek or lake, dipping bags into the water while trying not to get your feet wet as you balance various bladders and bottles on unhelpful rocks. But at least you don't have to keep track of a bunch of hoses.

Water filters are nice because they save you from the residual flavors and wait times of chemical treatments. They are impressively light for their size and guaranteed to last longer than a pack of tablets. However, they are also far more expensive than said pack of tablets, and could never hope to take up as little space in your pack. But the small crimes of being large and pricey are not my beef with water filters. My problem is the amount of TLC they require. If you accidentally place a pump's hose too close to a silty streambed, you can clog it with silt. Housed in a thoughtfully crafted case, the filter is designed to survive many drops and bangs, but if you expose it to freezing temperatures, its efficacy is permanently compromised. They are almost impossible to use in shallow creeks or cliffside springs. Their output often slows for mysterious reasons. They won't eat anything with bell peppers and they vape in the house. They're just a lot to deal with.

To save yourself some misery if you get a filter, keep in mind that they need to be backwashed or rinsed on a regular basis. If you forget to clean your filter at the end of a trip, you'll be very rudely reminded of this fact the next time you use it. I went hiking at an elevation of around 9000 feet in the Uinta-Wasatch Range in Utah one sunny September day, without acclimating at all from sea level carrying only one liter of water because "it's only a day hike," and also because sometimes I'm an idiot. I did, however, remember to bring my water filter. After slogging uphill for 5 miles, my lungs felt like they were filled with cobwebs, my water bottle was as dry as the air surrounding me, and I felt consumed by the kind of thirst depicted in movies where parched victims of a plane crash crawl desperately out of the ocean and onto the sand of a strange desert island. Eventually, after walking up what felt like an infinite hill, I arrived at a magnificent, sparkling mountain lake, nestled between titanic slabs of granite.

I thanked my morning self for remembering to pack my water filter, and eagerly crawled across a surfboard-shaped slab of granite toward the surface. With the silky water gently lapping at my shoes, I filled up the pouch of my squeeze bag, attached the filter, and excitedly began to squeeze the water into my water bottle—but nothing happened. I squeezed harder, and still no water came out of the filter. I panicked.

I suddenly and vividly remembered that I hadn't backwashed the filter the last time I used it, nor had I tested it that morning. Although I had brought the plunger device designed to backwash the filter, I had no clean water to use it. Panic sizzled through my body as I realized: I couldn't drink. I had to hike the entire five miles back to the trailhead at elevation without water. I screamed. Surely this was a trap. I was on a secret game show, and any minute now the curtain would come up and Drew Carey would come pat me on the back and hand me an entire flat of La Croix. I debated whether to stick my head into the lake and let the gods decide whether I got sick. Eventually (thirst is very motivating), I managed to put enough pressure on the bag to coax a trickle of water into my bottle. It took about twenty minutes—well really, it took forty minutes because I kept drinking from the bottle—but eventually my bottle filled up, and my swollen tongue reminded me never to do that again.

Anyway, if the idea of having to remember to carefully wash and preen your water filter after each trip sounds like too much hassle, there's another somewhat new water purification option, one that doesn't involve any pumping or squeezing: a tiny lightsaber of UV light that scrambles the DNA of everything inside your water bottle. What a satisfying concept. I'd probably be really happy with a UV purifier, but unfortunately it runs on batteries. It's bad enough my headlamp needs batteries; I'm too afraid to add another electronic liability to the list of things I bring outside. Plus, frankly, I've heard too many horror stories about them flat-out breaking in the middle of the backcountry, leaving their owners with the frustrating task of having to boil every drop they drink. (OK, I've heard one story. But honestly one is enough.)

There are times when it makes sense to buy inexpensive backpacking gear. Maybe you buy a non-brand-name pack, because you don't really care if one little strap breaks, or you get a used shirt, or a cheap aluminum pot. But now? Now is not that time. Do not cheap out on your water cleaning system. Whatever you buy, get it new and from a reputable company that accepts returns. The downside of cheaping out on clothing is maybe you're a little colder than you planned. The downside of cheaping out on a water filter is maybe you blow buttchunks into a hospital pan for three weeks. Spend the cash—you're worth it, my friend.

HOW TO MAKE WATER FUN

I feel like I was born under a lucky star to be as enamored with flat, tap water as I am. Or maybe it's just a sign that I have no taste and grew up kind of poor. If you prefer your daily ration of aqua with bright, snappy bubbles or sweet, crisp essences and/or you feel a little repulsed by the idea of drinking lake water treated with salty chemicals or filtered through plastic straws—you're not alone. The good news is there are hundreds of options to make backcountry water more interesting (dare I say, pleasurable), and mask the nasty flavors that filtering and purification leave behind. Science has yet to figure out how to put Topo Chico bubbles into a half ounce packet that promises to turn any Nalgene full of lukewarm water into a cool glass of your favorite fizzy water, but if you'll accept a tall, cool bottle of "B-Vitamin Blue Raspberry Rumble" as a consolation prize, you have options. In the backcountry, electrolyte mixes go from being something professional soccer players haphazardly splash over their immaculate bodies in commercials to being something practical for the rest of us schmucks to ingest.

One of my favorite things to do before a trip is go into REI and buy those GU tabs that only seasoned mountain bikers, rock climbers, and other people with the lean frames and musculatures of Olympians seem to deserve. I feel like I can see people staring at me—my fists full of little packets, along with my muffin top and squishy arms—and saying under their breath, "What is *she* using those for?" I always imagine I'd respond, "Sweating, bruh. I'm eating ten miles every day for breakfast next week. Do you think they have any more lemon-lime?" But of course no one ever says anything like this to me, as all the people in REI are really nice and no one actually cares what I'm doing, because they're preoccupied with their own lives.

The point is, adding an electrolyte replacement to your water is a good idea. These, plus your salty snacks and meals, help prevent the violently low possibility that you will drink too much water and develop hyponatremia (low blood sodium brought on by excessive water consumption), and more importantly, they replenish the potassium, chromium, magnesium, and other essential minerals you will very likely be losing while sweating (and might not get back from your diet). Supplements are everything. Try working out without vitamin B for a week. Then try it with vitamin B. I'm not a nutritionist; I'm just saying you notice whether you have this shit or you don't. Dropping some in your water is an easy way to get it.

If you're still feeling confused about how much you should drink, or how many water bottles you should take with you into the backcountry, the best way to figure this out is to deeply familiarize yourself with the terrain on your route beforehand. You need to get a map.

Chapter 8

MAPS
Discovering It's Easier to Find Your Way Out Here Than in Life

"Do you bring a compass with you?"
"No. But that's probably a good idea."
    —Two backpacking experts

I wish I could share some great revelation about why I choose to go where I go in the wilderness: That I'm the daughter of the fairy king and, if I don't come home periodically, he'll start a war between the realms of man and fae. Or that hiking is the secret to my magazine-cover bikini body, or the key to erasing my mind of toxic, pore-clogging stress and carb cravings in order to "be in the moment." I wish I could offer you some tale of my trials that would culminate neatly in a dazzling memoir about survival and self-actualization, landing me several sponsorships and an interview with Oprah. But I don't have that for you.

Instead I'm just the idiot who saw a photo and decided it was a good idea to spend $1,000 and hike fifty miles to say I saw it in person.

Flash backward in time to me, at age eighteen, lying on my mom's tan living room couch, staring into the middle distance, bored and directionless and frozen.[32] It was 2007, about eight months after my high school graduation. My brain was drenched in hormones and composting everything I'd just learned in school about how unfair the world is (plus, I guess, all the state capitals, and how to manually calculate a logarithm). I was staring into the metaphorical gray expanse that comes after something extremely promising has happened, and then you're on the other side of it, unsure what exactly happens next. I was drowning in so much ennui I could barely manage to raise one arm off the couch to open the oversize book, titled *Best Hikes of the World,* someone had left on the coffee table. I turned to a random page, not because I wanted to, but simply because I had nothing better to do and the whole world was going to hell and it wasn't like anything mattered anyway so why not read a book before we all died.

The picture took up two pages. A waterfall of golden sunshine was pouring onto a field of grass, off the page, and onto me. The sky was glacial blue, and rays of sunbeams pierced through a herd of puffed, vanilla clouds, their bodies breaking open with light. A basket of cherry-red flowers lined a long mahogany balcony, from which the photographer invited me to view the battle between the clouds and the sunbeams taking place in the sky. A thousand feet below the balcony, shadows snaked their way through a hunter-green valley, a thread of quicksilver water running between them, darting into the horizon.

It took just a second—as long as it takes to look at a photograph and feel something. In that moment, some part of me decided, or seemed to know, or seemed to want to know, that if I could get there—if I could just see this place in real life—everything that felt wrong now, everything that could feel wrong to an eighteen-year-old after graduation, everything that made me feel useless and desperate and as though—teetering on the cusp of adulthood and college and three waves of feminist theory—I had been judged and measured and despite my efforts would be found wanting . . .

---

32. This was right before smartphones became ubiquitous, so teenagers did sit around being bored.

would simply go away. Because this was heaven. And I wouldn't have to be me anymore. I would be an angel.

So, again, no real insight. Just pretty pictures. It's one way to pick out a trip, but if you prefer a slightly more thoughtful, less emotionally reactive process, I'd suggest beginning right at home. Find a photo or a story—even some gossip—something that makes you say, out loud and to an empty room, for whatever reason is inside of you, "Holy shit." That's your mark.

Now the chase begins.

RESEARCHING BACKPACKING ROUTES

The best way to learn about a backpacking route is to read a book about it. So let's talk about how you're going to look up everything on the internet.

Before the internet, backpacking information, I think, used to be a bit like Amish bread recipes—shared via word of mouth. Someone who knew the trail and what was needed to traverse it took another person there, who then learned the information and passed it on to someone else (adding a bit of their own experience and leaving some of the original out), and the cycle continued.

If you didn't know someone who could serve as your own personal trail guide, you read books—beautiful, tangible books, written with genuine love and deep care by vetted professionals who had earned the respect of their peers. These books were the standard for finding out whatever you wanted to know about any route at all. And they still exist. While today books have the misfortune of competing with that supposedly free encyclopedia of all information sitting in everyone's back pocket, they are, without question, the most reliable source of information about a wilderness area or backpacking trip. I always buy one to read up on a place before I visit, and strongly encourage you to do the same.

But, ah, the internet is free and vast and full of friendly people posting information that's up to date as of yesterday. You can find day-by-day blogs with detailed itineraries, calculate the exact distance and elevation gain between two landmarks, see recent photos of routes, and even find GPS tracks; in short, you can find what appears to be everything you need to know. Simply google the area you're looking for plus the words "backpacking routes" and a variety of private company blogs and nonprofit forums will eagerly raise their hands, offering to give you all the tools you need for your Perfect Outdoor Adventure™.

Some of you can probably sense where I'm going with this. We live in a brave new world with incalculable stores of free knowledge, which in turn allows us to lead each other, not even maliciously, into the illusion that we can know what we're getting into before we get into it. Wondering if you should clean your bathtub with Diet Coke? Google it. Not sure where you should take a first date out to dinner? Yelp it. Is that $2,000 guitar worth it? Find a video on YouTube of someone playing it. All of this information is ever ready, at your service, and free of charge. As a result, we are becoming less and less comfortable with uncertainty, because, well, we don't really have to be.

I am not above all this. With Ravenclaw reliability, I spend *hours* online while planning a route, researching seasonal conditions, and looking at photos and reviews from people who have been there already—even if I have a book about it. I hunt for this information like my life depends on it (because it kinda feels like it does), and after innumerable hours at this task, I become so confident I wonder what anyone ever did about anything before the blessed internet.

Then I get to the trailhead. The "clear" path I read about requires bush-whacking through poison oak. The "little stream" is a torrential, impass-able river. I learn with embarrassing clarity that HikerDude247's definition of "moderate difficulty" is much, much more generous than my own. The landscape isn't "tranquil mixed conifers"; it's matchsticks from last year's wildfire. Maybe it's also raining, and the area is experiencing an unseason-able cold snap. Sometimes (my favorite) the trail is missing altogether. Or maybe, maybe, by some miracle, everything actually goes as the reviews said it would. And then somebody steps on a snake.

Basically, it's never like the reviews I read, the photos I scrounged, or the YouTube videos I dug up. Or even on the rare, rare, rare chance it is all as described, how I feel when I'm there never quite matches how I thought I'd feel when I was sitting in a soft bed at home, lazily swiping through pho-tos of someone else's perfectly packaged adventure.

The thing about advice you read online is that it completely falls to shit once you enter the wilderness. That's because wilderness is by definition the antonym of civilization: it is unpredictable and unplanned—you don't always know what you're going to find. In fact, patience in the face of uncertainty may be one of the most profound lessons backpacking can teach you. At the end of the day, your plan is going to fall apart in either a big way or a small way. I promise. And that, weirdly, is what usually ends up being the adventure.

This isn't to say that internet research is useless, especially if paired with a book on the area. That would be as bad as saying it's all you need. The internet just needs to be navigated carefully.

Let's pretend you have a friend named Patsy. Patsy is a ravishing heiress with an IQ of 200 who spends her days winning physics prizes in Tokyo and throwing parties with Beyoncé in Geneva. She invented blockchain. She has a photographic memory. She's on the board of Uber and is also the top donor to the ACLU. The best part about Patsy is that she loves you, she's obsessed with your happiness, and she wants to give you *everything*. At the same time, and with equal intensity, she is a sociopath, a drunk, and a pathological liar. Approach the internet the way you would approach Patsy.

PICKING OUT A TRAIL

Chances are you might already have a trail in mind, as most people don't prep to go backpacking without a goal that can justify all this effort. But if no one has ever told you anything like "OH MY GOD you *haaaaave* to go to the Tetons in the spring. It's—dude—it's UH-MAAAAAAZING" and you are looking for some guidance, allow me to share my process.

You can start to generate an idea of where you want to go by picking up a book about the best backpacking routes in the park or forest you want to visit, or googling stuff like "best California mountains in spring" or "beginner backpacking trips in Wyoming." It's usually nice to first decide on the best season (since things like water sources, shade, and temperatures can vary wildly between seasons), an area not too far away from where you live (like eastern Utah, the Sierra Nevada, or the Catskills), the length of trip you'd like to take, and your physical abilities or limitations (beginner, good for kids, etc.).

You'll find a lot of different backpacking locations, managed by a lot of different agencies. Nearly all are government run and have the word "Park," "Forest," "Land," or "Service" in their names. It may appear that all of

America's wilderness is run under a single hunter-green and beige umbrella, but in fact, each of these organizations has a unique management style.

National parks, for example, contain the actual mountains and prairies they're singing about in "God Bless America." They are crowded, organized, expensive, well supplied, and *gorgeous*. They have entrance fees, hotels, paved roads, kiosks, and sometimes even Wi-Fi. Within their esteemed boundaries are some of America's most cherished landscapes, but they're also the kind of place where you are entitled to be offended if you can't find a vending machine that stocks Cheetos (both original and flamin' hot). The Grand Canyon, Yosemite, and Great Smoky Mountains are all national parks.

National forests, on the other hand, are the national parks' scruffy, neglected, banjo-twanging sister. They are less frequented, less expensive, and less developed. Someone once told me the official difference is that national parks are all about "preservation" and national forests are all about "conservation." Considering how often national forests sell logging rights to timber companies, I don't know how true that is. But I think the idea is that national parks are about preserving some part of quintessential American magnificence for future generations, and national forests are repositories for the trees we should probably keep around to combat climate change. This is an act. Don't let the quiet little sister fool you. Inside their undeveloped, unadvertised landscapes, American national forests contain some of the most intense, rapturous, and life-changing backpacking routes in the entire world.

Two other key differences between a national park and a national forest are the number of people you're likely to encounter while there and, correspondently, how chill the rangers are. Many backpacking routes that start in national parks are so aggressively famous that the National Park Service holds lotteries for the (required) permits, which you must enter up to a year in advance. Furthermore, national park rangers can be rather uptight—they have to be. They spend a disturbing amount of their time dealing with recalcitrant schoolchildren, teenagers trying to impress each other, and BASE jumpers. Their job is horrifically hard. People want to go into nature to feel rugged, light fires, and climb things without permits. But you can't do any of that in a national park, usually because someone did it once, got killed, and now it's a liability. By August, near the end of

America's camping season, national park rangers are exhausted, badgered, and definitely sick of your shit. If you see a park ranger on Labor Day, you better be either handing them a cookie or getting out of their way.

National forests, on the other hand, seem to operate on more of an optimistic "don't ask, don't tell" policy. They don't have a lot of general stores or entrance fees, and many of their roads are unpaved. (Frankly, I recommend that you avoid driving on any unpaved roads unless you have a high-clearance vehicle.[33]) However, what national forests lack in polish, they make up for in freedom: you can camp nearly anywhere, gather wood, shoot guns, and all but hook your guitar up to an amp and put on a Dolly Parton tribute concert for the squirrels. Backpacking routes that start in national forests rarely require permits beyond ones for parking, and those that do are virtually never popular enough to necessitate a lottery. I don't think I've ever met a ranger in a national forest, to be honest. I'm not 100 percent certain they exist. Just don't be an asshole, and you likely can continue to wonder if they exist too.

In addition to national parks and national forests, there are state parks and state forests: two little dreamers chanting "I think I can, I think I can, I think I can," while staring up at their older cousins, wondering when they'll be pretty enough to get federal funding too. State parks and forests tend to be quite small, so backpacking there, while not unheard of, tends to be less common. Where I live in the San Francisco Bay Area, two state parks offer backpacking camps, but they are so close to the suburbs that the waitlist to get a permit is longer than for midrange private daycare. In these smaller parks, you are usually better off base camping or car camping (if allowed), with pleasant day hikes in between.

Then there's Bureau of Land Management, or BLM, land. Its website describes its mission as everything from conserving land for recreational use to hosting land for mining and energy development—or for growing weed. OK, granted, my only real experience with BLM land is when I went backpacking through a part that overlapped with the "Emerald Triangle," an

---

33. See me, in Mendocino National Forest in northwestern California, bottoming out on a pock-marked, unpaved road in a sedan hatchback that a camp host said "would be fine," while my dashboard lights up like a Christmas tree and I start screaming.

unofficial zone of NorCal where for the past fifty years back-to-landers have been opening yoga studios, brewing kombucha, and growing insurrectionary amounts of marijuana.[34] Although inhabited mostly by peaceful, sunbaked hippies, many of the prayer-flag-draped homesteads you'll find up there also happen to be loaded with electric fences, rottweilers, semiautomatic shotguns, and fields of a drug known to induce paranoia.

One of the first backpacking trips Jeanne and I planned on our own was in the Emerald Triangle, as it also happens to house the Lost Coast: a misty, blustery, beach-hugging trail that runs along a gray-green seashore. It had been a year since we had finished the Team program in 2006, but we would still go visit the school occasionally to say hello to our former teachers Chuck and Patchen, and take them up on their perennial offer to borrow bear canisters and fleece pants from the stockroom. On one of these visits, Chuck asked politely about our itinerary. Hearing where we were going, he said, in his crackling voice with some uncharacteristic seriousness, "You're really going to want to heed the 'no trespassing' signs you'll see out there, OK?" We didn't quite know what he was talking about, but we dutifully nodded. In retrospect, I realize he wasn't so much afraid we'd run into Mary Jane. He was afraid we'd run into her dad.

In sum, if you want a little more hand-holding (and to see something so beautiful even Republican politicians sometimes agree to keep funding it), you should really think about going to a national park. If you want a little more space and privacy, aim for a national forest. If you want to commit a heist, head for BLM land.

There are at least ten other classifications of places where you can backpack, usually run by the National Forest Service, National Park Service, or the Bureau of Land Management, which are in turn run by the United States Forest Service and the Department of the Interior. Sometimes various combinations of these groups team up to manage things like national conservation areas or the National Trails System. Land management agencies are America's version of British peerage: The details are dizzying, but it invariably boils down to someone in a khaki vest telling you to "pack in what you pack out."

---

34. It's also where I was born.

WHAT'S IN A NAME?

Don't ever be thrown by the name of a route or wilderness area when choosing a backpacking destination. That cherry-flowered paradise in my mom's *Best Hikes of the World* coffee-table book—the one that hypnotized me out of $1,000 for a trip to Europe at the age of eighteen—is a village in the Swiss Alps called Gimmelwald. That sounds like the name of a balrog you have to slay in order to save the kingdom's last hobbit but nothing could be farther from the truth; it's a sunny little village whose economy, as far as I could tell, ran on kindness, sunshine, and cheese.

So when you come across Tragedy Spring, Jackass Mountain, and Deadman Summit in your research (all real, all in California), I encourage you not to judge them by the names that dysentery-afflicted puritan settlers in a religious panic christened them in the eighteenth century. Desolation Wilderness, for example, is a triumph of natural beauty, so long as you're viewing it with a full canteen and some snacks.

Equally magical experiences can be had in all these places. There is an obvious temptation to assume that national parks must be the loveliest, followed by national forests, state parks, state forests, and BLM land. But this hierarchy of beauty does not actually exist. I have experienced the same level of awe watching blankets of fog embrace fields of redwoods along the Lost Coast as I have staring up at the famous Half Dome's glacial glory in Yosemite Valley.

Whether it's in a park, in a forest, or on BLM land, once you have a route picked out, you'll invariably come across conflicting reviews on the internet. The best thing about backpacking books is that they don't have reviews—it's just one voice, who genuinely wants to help you have a good and safe time. Internet reviews have no such altruistic motive, just buckets and buckets of opinions.

Reading a backcountry review is like hearing a prophecy: it's not that it's untrue; it's that what *isn't* being said is what will get you into trouble. But there is still a whole mess of information that can be gleaned from a trail review, just from context and how things are said. For example, if you find a route because it's the top hit on a Google search, the highest-rated route on AllTrails, or mentioned even once in a Lonely Planet guidebook, you can be pretty confident that the place will have well-defined trails, convenient campsites, and stunning vistas. You will also probably find yourself waiting in a line of ten people to take a selfie at one of those vistas. If a particular route has five solid stars, 180 comments, and 700 photos, you are going to be sharing it with all the other people who read those reviews (not to mention the trash of the hundreds of other people who visited but didn't write a review because they didn't want to "spoil the place").

But don't despair. These are the ingredients of a great first backpacking trip. You'll still get all that wonderful self-actualization through carrying a heavy bag for miles around a mountain along with the feeling of being a far cry from home (without actually being a far cry from someone who could help you if you broke a leg). Plus, these routes are usually popular for a good reason: you're going to see something jaw-dropping, even if you're standing shoulder to shoulder with a stranger to see it.

I used to really hate the idea of crowds—I didn't drive one hundred miles into the middle of nowhere to practice "sharing." Not only did they ruin my craving for an authentic experience with the wild (which is, of course, just the mountain and me, brooding by a cliffside, having really deep thoughts about the human condition, and maybe inventing a secret handshake with a bear), crowded parks have also become a bit dangerous. As the world gets more intimate with easily transmitted diseases, parks, swollen with nature-hungry kids raised on screens looking to "get away from it all," can become breeding grounds for infectious outbreaks.

When I visited Torres del Paine in 2017, this backpacker's bucket-list destination was so choked with people that Jeanne and I found ourselves squeezing shoulders past other hikers every ten to twenty minutes. Each campground was a village of brightly colored nylon mushroom domes, with the floating lights of headlamps dancing about. The toilets were also overflowing with shit, and we heard a rumor that there was an E. coli outbreak in the park. We treated all our water twice and drenched our hands in sanitizer every time we touched a door handle. I was more afraid of the outhouse at Refugio Gray than I had ever been of a bathroom in an overcrowded Starbucks or sketchy inner-city McDonald's. Three years later, when parks across the globe were shut down due to the COVID-19 pandemic, I immediately understood why.

If a good reputation meant big crowds, I convinced myself the reverse must also be true: a dearth of information about a place was, in fact, an indicator of its true greatness, which would be revealed solely unto me if I simply had the bravery to go there alone.

Thusly, I flung myself into woody places that had no online reviews, and no books written about them, feeling brilliant and witty and all but banging pots and pans together to let the forest fairies know I was fully available for abduction or at least some afternoon tea.

Instead, my reward was walking among foul, wilting weeds, swimming in rivers choked with worms and algae, and camping amid literal clouds of mosquitoes. That is how I learned that just because a place isn't written about very often doesn't mean it's an unspoilt gem you'll have all to yourself. It could mean what it appears to mean: it's a shitheap, and people have been avoiding it for a reason.

If you go into nature seeking Yeats-worthy magic and Thoreau levels of solitude, I'd suggest looking for trails with good reviews—but just not very many. Maybe one or two photos, so you can get a feel for at least (part) of the landscape, and one or two actual comments. Consider how far away the trail is from a big city (the closer it is, the more popular it will be). Or, try to bribe an experienced backpacker into telling you their secret solitude getaway (hint: we'll do just about anything for an ultralight Patagonia down parka). Most books written about backpacking in a certain area will also tell you how crowded it's likely to get by season (again, guidebook writers tend to have more empathy for your backpacking goals in general).

Either way, once you find a route or area that seems like it'll be the right level of crowded, the right level of hardcore, and the right number of days, you're not done yet. You're not going to take Patsy's word for it. It's time to confirm all of that information for yourself by plotting your course on a topographic map.

DECIDING BETWEEN PAPER AND DIGITAL MAPS

I have tried so many times to go hiking without a proper topographic map. These decisions have gotten me lost in a place called Mount Diablo—twice.

One time, I decided to use a map I had found online through an incredibly nifty site called OpenCycleMap. This site shows every trail that does or could possibly exist on any given piece of land in the world, at any zoom level—for free. Holy shit. The catch was, the website didn't allow you to print or download anything from this other-worldly font of trail wisdom. I didn't want to rely on my phone to access the site—data service is unreliable at best in most quality wildernesses, and I didn't want to risk running out of battery, either. So I wrote down the directions on a piece of paper as if I were jotting down the steps to get to my aunt Madge's house off MapQuest in 1999. "Turn left at the first junction, then right on the Jefferson Trail, go four miles, turn right again," etc.

The day started with me eagerly clutching these country-road-style directions and smirking at how I had outsmarted the system. It ended at five in the afternoon with me panting, confused, and on the verge of tears, as the sun was setting and I had absolutely no idea where I was.

The thing about trails is that they are not roads. They aren't even backroads. Once you get on one, it's usually embarrassingly easy to stay on it, but finding the fucking thing can be a different task entirely. They are not often reliably marked, and trailheads that are clearly shown on a map can be overgrown and barely visible in person. This makes writing down instructions like "turn right on the Jefferson Trail" impressively useless, unless you also have a step counter, a GPS, or an app that's tracking your every move.

I tried using the AllTrails app a few times. My punishment the first time was getting lost in a parking lot near a redwood reserve for forty-five minutes while looking for a trailhead the app swore I was right on top of. I finally found the trail, only to get lost again thirty minutes later, at a T intersection my app refused to agree we were standing right in front of. I repeated this experience again in Umpqua National Forest in Oregon, and for a third time in the foothills outside of Yosemite National Park, before I finally gave up.

The average review for this app is five stars. I'm not saying this is clear evidence that I'm an idiot, but I'm also not *not* saying AllTrails is actually run by a Russian hacking group attempting to lure Americans to their deaths by getting them lost in their own natural recreation areas.

Before the ubiquity of smartphones with built-in GPS, handheld, dedicated GPS devices were popular in the hiking world. Many hikers still swear by them. But, for most folks, the standalone GPS is overkill; there are so many apps out there that can turn your phone into a multitool of backcountry badassery, you probably don't need a Garmin brick on top of everything else you're about to buy.

The exception would be if you're going completely off-trail—bush-whacking—which is entirely more badass. For this, you would require not only a GPS device but a compass, a machete, some face paint, and/ or a woman named Sacagawea. Imagine trampling flowers and hacking vines as you forge your own way through old-growth forests, hunting your own food, making sooty fires everywhere, and turning your nose up at any helpful "trails" designed to protect the region from people exactly like you. What a hero.

In my opinion, the best apps are those that essentially function as mere digital platters for actual topographic maps, like ViewRanger, Cal-Topo, Green Trails, or NGS maps. Most of these work in tandem with your phone's GPS (assuming your GPS works where you're going), allowing you to watch the progress of the little blue dot on the trail (that's you), a real-time, reassuring sign that you haven't colossally fucked up yet. Down-loading maps to your phone so you can use them offline, is also particularly helpful on a day hike, where pulling out something the size of a newspaper can feel a bit slapstick.

However, at the end of the day, the only thing you really need to orient yourself on a backpacking trip in my lazy, Luddite opinion is the will to stay on the trail, some idea of where the sun is, and a paper topographic map. That's it. I feel like I should also tell you a compass is useful, because that seems like something a responsible person would tell you. However, in my fifteen years of backpacking, even when lost, I have never once thought, "Gee, I wish we had a compass right now." (But this may be evidence of my poor navigation skills more than anything else). All I know is that if you make a point to stay on the trail, know how to read your map, and have the ability to identify large objects in the distance, you can backpack. This is probably the root of why, no matter what anyone says to me about how "amazing" or "brave" I must be for striding into the untamed wilds, I'll never feel like backpacking makes me a badass. I just walk down the only dirt road visible for forty miles and occasionally stop to take pictures next to pretty flowers. The only real difference between my backpacking trips and your grandmother's garden tours is access to flush toilets.

Anyway. I'd be foolish to tell you your phone is verboten in the wilderness, but I have two reasons for believing the paper topographic map is superior. First, your smartphone is a wuss. It hates temperature swings, moisture, and getting banged around; the wilderness is the quintessential antithetical environment for a small electronic device. Furthermore, smartphones run on electricity, which means carrying battery packs and worrying about keeping things topped up (and being in very serious trouble if you forget). They don't always work in valleys or canyons where access to the sky is limited. They can slip out of your hand, get clogged with dirt, are generally not waterproof without a special case, and in all other ways behave as the star of the black-and-white opening to an infomercial. Both a map made of paper and a map on your phone can guide you. The difference is that one was designed for this exact task, while the other is being stored on a device powered by a battery.

Second, past the logistics of caring for the particular, delicate baby kitten that is your phone, there's the concept of "unplugging" to contend with.

When I was nine, I had a cluster of Tamagotchis that I felt a great deal of responsibility for. My mother, an avid hiker, frequently threw me in the car along with her fanny pack and Nalgene for a day hike up a local mountain. On one morning, we were marching along under a pretty blue sky next to fields of coyote brush and manzanita, and I pulled out one of my little chirpers to give it a snack or a bath or whatever the algorithm had determined it needed at ten in the morning on a Sunday. My mother did a quiet double take.

"You shouldn't bring those out here," she said, not unkindly.

"Why?" I asked back, defensively, as if to say "shouldn't mothers support mothers?"

She brushed off my question with a wave of her hand and said, "Because that's not why we go out here." She kept walking and left me to figure out the rest.

To this day, I have a weird thing about pulling out my phone in the wilderness. Yes, it's probably some leftover complex about not wanting to disappoint my mother. But also, every time I do it, I can't help feeling like

I just pulled out a crucifix at a Wiccan ceremony. Didn't I come out here to turn off my phone, recharge my retinas with long-distance vision, and avoid false blue light? Am I not, then, betraying the greater goal of reconnecting with nature: to unplug?

Look, I'm not going to sit here and pretend all technology is evil; a great deal of "unnatural" technology gets me through my backpacking trips. (Nylon isn't exactly spun from silkworms, is it?) My phone's meager GPS has rescued me from walking in circles on day hikes and helped me find a snowed-over trail more than once. I've also been tramping on slugs and caterpillars while up to my hips in ferns—unable to find the trail I had been on just seconds ago—asking why fate made me such an ignoramus as to forget to bring my phone so I could find my way back home.

However, the idea of taking all this time off work, driving away from the comforts of home and out into the middle of nowhere, and then hiking to an even more remote location in order to *check my phone* feels like some kind of backward nightmare. I don't even like doing it on day hikes, which can serve as a truly fantastic and low-maintenance way to unplug.

If you are planning a lot of off-trail hijinks, or are so intent on knowing *exactly* where you are on the trail at *every* single moment that you are willing to spend extra money and carry extra weight for that sense of security, you're welcome to use a GPS device or GPS-enabled smartphone on the trail. Truly. But you'll still have to contend with anxiety when your GPS tracking inevitably starts lagging or you realize you forgot to download the latest version of its software.

Or you can just buy and learn how to read a paper topographic map. It never fails to feel like so much less work.

ACQUIRING A TOPOGRAPHIC MAP

Now that I've thrown all my wilderness trail app startup sponsorship opportunities out the window, let's talk about how to actually acquire one of these paper topographic maps:

1. Go the ranger station of the wilderness area you are interested in, when they are open, and on a day when they have topographic maps in stock.

2. Realize this is impossible.
3. Do an internet search to determine which agency runs the park or forest you want to visit. Look for a topographic map on that agency's website.
4. Realize the website is 100 percent unnavigable garbage.
5. Return to your search engine of choice and type in the name of the agency, the name of the park or forest you want to visit, and the words "wilderness map." For example, "NFS Shasta-Trinity wilderness map." That should take you within one or two clicks of the page on the agency's website where the actual map is for sale (or sometimes available to download free).
6. If you skipped steps one through five and went straight to Amazon or eBay, don't hit "buy" yet—first make sure you are looking at the most up-to-date version. The best way to do this is to buy directly from the wilderness service store. Trails change. Volcanoes erupt. Areas become impassable due to fallen trees, new rivers, or efforts to restore wildlife. Mountains can and do move.
7. Go back to the wilderness agency's service store, and buy the map. Give Ranger Rick twelve dollars. No one is funding the forest service anymore. Did you see that website? They need the money.

When I proudly described this process to Jeanne, she said, "You can also just walk into REI and buy one. They're open until 9:00 p.m. Are you really writing a book on this?"

Anyway. No matter what method you choose, make sure the map you get is a topographic map. Any backpacking or wilderness map that advertises itself as such *should* be a topographic map, but it's best to check before you buy. In addition to topographic lines, it will likely have trail names, boundary lines, and water sources—key to planning your trip.

USING A TOPOGRAPHIC MAP TO PLAN YOUR TRIP

If you've never read a topographic map before, it's really not so difficult. It just requires a pinch of patience and a good eye (seriously—if you're farsighted, you should go grab your glasses for this next part).

A topographic map basically looks like a regular map somebody doodled on while they were bored during math class. Open it up and you'll see a sea of faded, squiggly lines overlaying the terrain. The squiggly lines are technically called "contour lines." Each contour line represents a specific elevation, or in other words, everything along that line, throughout the entire map, is the same height above sea level. Some of the lines will be bold, and have their elevation written on them. You'll have to infer the elevation of the other lines by counting down, or up, from the bold lines. To do this, you'll need to determine the "contour interval," or difference in elevation between two contour lines, on the map's legend. Usually the contour interval is 80 feet, 100 feet, or 300 feet.

For example, let's say we're looking at a map whose contour interval is 100 feet. Following one bold line, we see that it represents an elevation of 2,500 feet. That means the lines on either side of it represent 2,400 and

2,600 feet, respectively. To know which way is up and which way is down, find other bold lines and see if their elevation is greater or lesser than 2,500 feet.

How does this information help you plan your trip? Let's say the area on the map you're planning to travel through shows contour lines spread far apart over many miles. You can read that as an easy, flat walk without dramatic elevation changes. You'll likely be able to cruise across the area at your normal walking pace. On the flipside, if your trail crosses a bunch of squiggly lines packed together like a clump of spaghetti, that's the day you're going to learn about knee pain.

So, pull out your map, and inhale that nice, new-map smell. Now let's figure out the distance between your start point and end point, how far you'll be traveling each day, and where you'll be getting your water.

Estimating How Much This Is Going to Hurt

I know some people who wing it like true bohemians and march off into the forest with no plan, no map, and a bellyful of faith that the wind and the stars will just kind of blow them where they need to go. Granted, if you're going somewhere with copious water sources, and you don't need to return to a job at a specific time, that's a super available choice. But if water is a bit scarce on the trail, or if you're like most of us and need to know when exactly you'll be back home, it's prudent to have an itinerary that covers your total travel distance, per day travel distance, and water sources. It will ensure you pack enough food, don't shrivel up like a desiccated lizard in the sun, and get back to your day job on time.

Many famous backpacking routes outlined in books and on popular blogs provide specific details as to what landmarks you'll be traveling between each day, such as, "Day 1: Steaming Valley to Dicks Peak. Day 2: Dicks Peak to Rumpus Gorge," etc. Even if you are following a route this detailed, it's still a good idea to compare what you've been told with what's on the topographic map. This will ensure that you can hike the route as specified, and also that nothing has changed since the author of the blog or book wrote their recommendations.

Let's try it together. On your map, find the trail that connects Steaming Valley to Dicks Peak. A line that represents a trail on a map is usually a

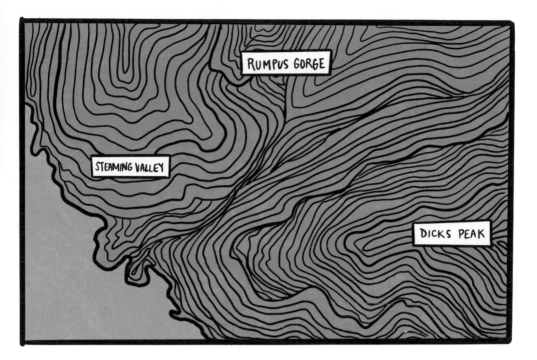

bold, dashed line, but check your legend to be sure. Some maps will have really helpful numbers along the trail line, telling you the mileage between two points. You can add them up to get the total mileage between that day's starting point and end point. This makes things pretty easy. But not all wilderness maps work this way, and sometimes you have to figure out the mileage yourself.

To do this, look for the scale in the legend that shows what a certain distance on the map equals in real life. In this example, our legend shows one inch on the map is equal to one mile in real life. I'm a fan of taking a piece of string, or, if I can't find any string because my craft drawer is a chaos pit, the middle segment of my pinky finger, and comparing it with the scale. More often than not, my pinky will register an even mile. Then I walk my pinky finger down the trail, counting out loud like a kindergartener, to determine how many miles are between Steaming Valley and Dicks Peak (always round up to be safe).

Let's say you end up with eight miles between the two points. Can you do eight miles in a day? Does that seem like too much? Too little? Actually you have no idea yet! Mileage is only half the equation—you still need to find the elevation change along those miles.[35]

To figure out the elevation change between our day's starting point and end point, we're going to check the contour interval on the map.

But first, let me tell you about a time I didn't do that. I was planning a trip to the foggy, wildflower-strewn hills of Big Sur, using a map that, I had assumed without checking, had a contour interval of 100 feet. I planned a whole trip around this assumption, which a few weeks later, resulted in my running completely out of water halfway up the summit of Cone Peak at one in the afternoon, with the June sun reflecting off white stones and suffocating me like I was the Pillsbury Doughboy trapped in an oven of my own hubris. The mountain kept going up, up, up—so much higher than I'd thought possible—until, finally, I collapsed on the ground under the only tree for miles, and began to cry. Not that "crying because something hurts" crying; it was that "crying because the world has betrayed me and it's not my fault" crying.[36] I kept checking my map, not understanding. "We're doomed. I've killed us," I told my boyfriend. "This can't possibly be the right way. It's not possible." Then, realizing the next water source wasn't for four more miles—and the only way to get through this was to summit the mountain and get to the stream on the other side—I put my pack back on, lifted myself off the ground, and continued to march onward, hoping death was too annoyed by my outburst to kill me.

Finally, after a few hours, we crossed the summit, descended to the stream, splayed ourselves in the shade of some poplar trees, and drank so much water my abdomen swelled like a balloon. Coming out of my stupor, I reached, for the millionth time that day, for the map that had surely betrayed me.

It hadn't. I had simply read it wrong.

---

35. If anyone told you there would be no math in this sport, they were lying.
36. This is the same way toddlers cry in the grocery store when they are told they cannot have Lucky Charms.

ONE MILE = ONE HOUR

I was taught one backcountry mile is equal to one hour of trail time. To advanced hikers, professional athletes, or people who have really perfected their weekday "I'm late for my shift" walk, this ratio will feel insane.

But walking in the backcountry with a pack on is very different from walking in your neighborhood, along city sidewalks, or on a treadmill. Once you factor in the weight on your back, the weather, the hills, and the breaks you'll be taking, one mile per hour starts to look pretty reasonable. I'm not going to sugarcoat this: Walking uphill all day with a sixty-pound backpack *suuuuucks*. It will make you question all your decisions. It will make you hate yourself. It will make you hate me. But then you'll get to the top of the thing and everything will be worth it (and also you'll be a little high on endorphins).

Some days you will be mostly hiking over flat land and then, yes, you will very likely go faster than one mile an hour. I have read accounts of people traversing the Pacific Crest Trail who easily blow past twenty miles per day, and I'm dutifully impressed by this. But I don't think it's super realistic for new backpackers, without ultralight gear, who haven't been hiking nonstop for the past three months.

If you aren't a super avid hiker, or if this is your first backpacking trip, stick with the one-mile-to-one-hour rule. Why? Because the worst thing that'll happen is you walk faster than you planned and you get to camp early with hours and hours to laze about in the sun, swim in a lake, or meditate on the clouds. The thing that sucks is getting to camp late, ashamed that you didn't do as much as you thought you could, and having to cook dinner and set up your tent by the spastic flicker of a headlamp.

If you don't like my rule of thumb but you also don't know your walking pace yet, the best thing to do is experiment with some day hikes. Put on a sixty-pound pack, and go see how long it takes to complete a seven-mile hike. Then do it again, but on a trail that also gains 2,000 feet in elevation, and see how long that takes.

Does that sound like too much work? Yes? Then just follow the rule of thumb.

My eyebrows floated off my face as I realized the topographic lines on the map were actually in 300-foot contour intervals, not 100-foot intervals. Everything, every climb up a hill, every descent into a valley, was going to be three times harder than I had originally planned. Could I even do this? (I started crying again.)

So don't be like me. Check your contour intervals ahead of time. They are the key to knowing what something is going to *feel* like. And thus how to prepare for it effectively.

Back to our example map, which has 100-foot intervals. Let's follow the squiggly lines the trail crosses between Steaming Valley and Dicks Peak. You'll notice the starting elevation at Steaming Valley is 1,000 feet, and, looking farther up the map, you'll notice the elevation at Dicks Peak is 3,100 feet. That means you'll gain a total of 2,100 feet of elevation while walking between those two points. This is called net elevation and, hooray, it's easy math! But what does net elevation actually mean? Honestly, not a ton, because nothing is ever a straight shot unless you're literally climbing up a mountainside. Your trail probably has a bunch of ups and downs along the way that you'd need to account for to get a true picture of what your day will look like.[37]

If you look closely at the numbers on the elevation lines along the route, you'll see that there are places where the contour lines bunch together, and the elevation descends. Then, some distance later, you'll see them bunch together again where the elevation ascends. Congratulations, you just found a valley! In fact, it looks like there is a ribbon of blue running through it.

Planning Your Water Fill-Ups

Most maps use solid blue lines to indicate reliable rivers and finger-print-size bubbles to represent lakes. As you're planning your route, ensure it crosses one of these reliable bodies of water every day—there would also ideally be one near each place you plan to camp at night. Dashed blue lines are sometimes used to indicate seasonal water sources that might not be there year-round. Always double-check your legend, as April's surging river can become October's leaky faucet.

---

37. Some people sum up every foot of loss and gain between two points to get a complete picture of the elevation changes they will encounter. It is, technically, the best way to determine how difficult a day is going to be. I don't usually do this, but I also follow the lazy one-mile-per-hour rule, which grants me all the slack I want. (I'm not in a hurry—are you?)

If you're reading an online account about where someone else stopped for water on a trip, definitely check the time of year they visited. Some routes have you stumbling over rivers and creeks and lakes every half hour, in which case you can all but carry a tin cup with you. Other routes, such as those that traverse deserts or plains, might only cross one body of water per day, so you really have to think about when you're filling up, and what part of your day that is.

However, most backpacking routes *are* backpacking routes because they travel near or across bodies of water at least once a day, and land you next to one at night for easy refreshment. If your map has backcountry campsites marked on it, you'll probably notice most of them are situated a few hundred feet away from a river or lake. Camping near a blue dot, line, or bubble on a map makes it easier to start and end the day without having to worry about water, and it's often nice to give your dear, hardworking feet a soak after hiking for miles. So, while it's not required, do yourself a favor and aim to camp near a river or lake each night.

In our example, we found a river in a little valley that cuts between Steaming Valley and Dicks Peak, which is a great place for a midday fill up. Now let's look at the next day, the route between Dicks Peak and Rumpus Gorge. You can see a stream near Dicks Peak, so you can fill up there in the morning, but—oh, look—there's no water again until Rumpus Gorge.

That isn't necessarily cause for *alarm*, but it is cause for pause. It means you'll have to carry all the water you'll be drinking that day with you when you leave Dicks Gorge. To figure out if that's a disaster waiting to happen, let's use our string (or middle pinky segment) to determine the distance between Dicks Peak and Rumpus Gorge. We find that it's nine miles. There is one sharp ascent of about 300 feet over the first half mile, and then it's mostly flat until you start climbing a peak over the last mile, another 800 feet (which is nothing to sneeze at, if you're at my level of fitness, anyway).

Now consider the time of year. Maybe you'll have a hot July sun floating over you the whole way. Add all of that up, and you realize that last mile is going to be quite hard. Instead of packing only two water bottles, you decide to pack four, so you can actually carry all the water you need from the stream at Dicks Peak.[38] Will you die if you don't? No, probably not. Will you be unnecessarily uncomfortable? Yeah, probably. Won't more water make your pack heavy? Yes, but never worry about water weight. Water weight moves fast—remember, "it's better in you than on you." If you bring an extra water bottle, there's a very good chance that at mile eight a sweaty, tired, sunbaked you will raise a cup to the sky in honor of trip-planning you, for being so gosh darn thoughtful.

FINDING A PLACE TO CAMP

Once you have located your water sources and planned your start and end points for each day, it's time to find a site to pitch your tent. At least sometimes you'll need to find campsites on your own. If you're in a heavily used park (like Yosemite or Torres del Paine), the agency in charge may insist you sleep in a designated backcountry campsite. These will almost always be marked on the map, and you'll know them when you see them in the field: a patch of land that looks starkly flat and unusually barren of flora (almost like a succession of people have pitched a tent there). Sometimes designated backcountry campsites have small shelters—essentially wooden shacks—designed to help protect you from particularly atrocious weather (such as on the Appalachian Trail). They may even have outhouses nearby, to prevent an influx of people from digging a thousand catholes and making the whole place smell like a pine-scented toilet.

If you're backpacking in a less popular wilderness area, the agency in charge may not require you to sleep in an official backcountry campsite, and there may not be any listed on the map. This is where the art of dispersed camping comes in. "Dispersed camping" is shorthand for "inventing your own campsite," assuming you're so far in the boonies there's nothing developed already. However, I have almost never had to do this, and you probably won't have to either. This is because, even if a campsite isn't officially listed on a backcountry map, there is almost

---

38. This is a great time to consider getting collapsible water bottles, so you can fold them up when not in use.

always an unofficial one established by previous campers, especially near bodies of water or notable landmarks.

Say you run into a river that crosses the trail six miles from your starting point. You might notice a few oddly barren, flat patches of dirt tucked behind some trees about two hundred feet from the water and one hundred feet from the trail. That, my friend, is a dispersed backcountry campsite. Or maybe twenty miles in there's an iconic lake, the only one around for miles. I can almost guarantee, if you circumnavigate the shoreline, you will find evidence of campsites past about two hundred feet from the water: unnaturally smooth patches of ground, a circle of charred stones, a seat-sized rock someone has clearly dragged over. It's best to use these "campsites" when you find them, not only to limit impact on the land, but because, frankly, it's much easier than making your own. Someone probably already cleared away most of the debris that would stick into your back at night, removed any dead trees or boulders that could fall on you while sleeping, and found a way to take advantage of one of the better views around.

You might see some backcountry campsites that are closer to a river or lake than the LNT mandated 200 feet; if you can, choose a site that is farther away from the shoreline. You'll not only score bonus points with the

SLEEPING IN DITCHES

I could have saved myself countless sleepless nights in the backcountry if someone had just told me not to sleep in a ditch. Think of cold air like water. The lower you go, the colder it will most likely be. This is why it's a good idea to avoid sleeping in dry riverbeds, valleys, or anything resembling a bowling gutter. Moving your tent even a few feet higher up a slope can make the difference between thirty-two and thirty-seven degrees.

Avoiding the lowest point in a valley or river canyon is also a great way to ensure you aren't swept away in a flash flood during the night. But most of the time, it's enough to avoid waking up with ice on your sleeping bag, wondering why the hell your friends (those bastards) who slept only twenty feet away from you (and two or three feet higher) did not.

Lorax, but sleeping farther away from water is also warmer and reduces the odds that wildlife will pass by your tent (and sniff around your camp) in the middle of the night.

For the perfect backcountry campsite, you have to find a place with a rather magical combination of ingredients: it's near water (but not closer than two hundred feet); it's near the trail (but farther than one hundred feet); it isn't in a wash; it's relatively flat; it's protected from wind; it's spacious enough to set up your cooking area, your cleaning area, and your sleeping area the recommended one hundred feet from each other; and widowmaker trees or rocks aren't about to fall on you. It's a rather particular list, and successfully following it—ensuring you stay safe and limit your impact on land and water—is seriously challenging and can sometimes feel impossible after a long day of hiking. Most backcountry campsites, either official or unofficial, have already ticked these boxes. In short, the people who made them have done the reconnaissance for you. These campsites are great. Use them.

To some, dispersed camping is less of a fallback and more of an opportunity to pay ritual homage to their great-great-grandfather's pioneer roots, and they smack their lips at the prospect of cutting down live branches and smashing down the understory to create the perfect scene. We all have our hobbies. However, inventing your own campsite is something you should only do as a last resort. Comfortable, natural campsites are difficult to find and do not disappear quickly once they are made. In many national parks, dispersed camping is forbidden and you should expect a handsome fine if you're caught doing it. I avoid it as much as possible and it doesn't make me feel any less hardcore.

MAKING MISTAKES

So what happens if you make a mistake? You did all this planning, but you're new at reading topographic maps. Maybe you end up misinterpreting contour lines, overlooking a junction, missing your landmarks, and overshooting the day's end point.

A great place to practice reading topographic maps is on a day hike close to home. The stakes are much lower, so you can make errors with fewer dire consequences. If I had practiced before going to Big Sur, for example, maybe I wouldn't have had a conversation with death under a tree on Cone Peak. Like with all your tools and gear, it's better to practice reading maps closer to home than pick up a skill your life depends on right before you head out on foot to a place with no highways or cell service. But even experienced people make mistakes.

When I was nineteen, Jeanne and I went on our fifth backpacking trip together along the Paria River, a slot canyon in Utah. The thirty-eight-mile trail threads between two rock walls the color of a lion's fur, at times expanding far enough apart to fit a house, and at other times narrowing so minutely they pressed against our skin as we walked by. The Paria River was constantly beneath our feet, flowing past boulders the size of bedrooms and quicksand puddles, which occasionally tested our ability to remain calm under pressure. The only landmarks were springs patched with green that spurted water sheepishly out of the canyon walls, petroglyphs made by Native peoples long ago, and places graced with the strikingly creative names first uttered by dehydrated Mormon women upon encountering them two hundred years ago ("Lonely Dell," for example). We had a pretty good idea of where we were (Jeanne had bought the map and planned our route on it while I gave second opinions like "that sounds about right" through mouthfuls of Pop-Tarts) and were having a good time.

On the third day, we ran into a large, organized group of middle-aged backpackers. We stopped and chatted pleasantly about water sources, the weather, and the distance to certain landmarks or campsites, as backpackers often do when they cross paths with each other on the trail. And then I made the mistake of asking, "Do you think the spring water is safe to drink without treating?" (I left out the fact that Jeanne had already been drinking it untreated, despite my stomping insistence that I wouldn't help her if she got giardia.)

My question gave a tall, stubble-beard man in his late forties an opening to approach us, invoke the fact that he was an ex-marine, size up Jeanne in her Care Bear–colored hiking dress and me in my ten-dollar running shorts, and decide we needed help. He told us that not only should we not drink the spring water untreated, but my water purification system (iodine) was grossly inappropriate. When we told him our backpacking teacher said the iodine would be fine, he proclaimed that "it doesn't kill anything" and gave us some of his chlorine tablets with an air of *You're welcome. This oughta keep you from getting killed for two more days.*

He then asked us where we thought we were. We pulled out our map and pointed. When we explained why we thought we were at this part of the trail, he simply waved his hand, pointed at a cluster of rocks, and told us where we "really" were, which was ten miles behind where we thought we were. Then he took off.

We stood in the river, clutching our map and the chlorine tabs, feeling more lost than we ever had before in our lives. Jeanne turned to me and called him an asshole, but we both somehow decided he was right. He must be right. We were nineteen, and he was an adult. With testicles.

That day we hiked for hours and hours and hours to make up for our missing ten miles. We had planned to reach a particular landmark that day, and we were sure (or rather, the ex-marine was sure) we hadn't passed it yet. We marched hard, wearily whipping past everything around us. At sunset, exhausted, we collapsed into the golden hour, set up our tent right next to the trail (a huge LNT faux pas), crawled into our sleeping bags, and sighed.

As darkness swelled over the desert, we whispered to each other about where we thought we were and whether we were horribly lost. How much food we had. Whether there were axe murderers outside. How surely if we were hidden in the tent, they wouldn't see us, because that was how tents worked.

The next morning, we prepared for another grueling day making up for lost time. And within thirty minutes, we were at a trailhead.

I blinked. Jeanne blinked. We were done. We had finished the hike a full day faster than we'd planned. We'd blown past the landmark we'd been looking for. Testicles was wrong; we'd known exactly where we were all along, and booked it for nothing.

We got in the car, rolled the windows down, turned up the radio on a German reggae band called Seeed that Jeanne had recently discovered, and drove into town for Dairy Queen.

Maps rarely lie, but humans do—to ourselves and to each other. You don't have to be perfect. Just stay on the trail, know where your water is, and keep your chin up. Even if you're a little wrong, or someone makes you think you're wrong, you're probably going to be fine. Yes, even if you cry a little first.

Chapter 9

HYGIENE
Or, Complete Lack Thereof

"I've learned that my natural scent is wild turnip."
    —A backpacking expert

It was nine in the morning. The sun was shimmering through droplets of fog, giving the air a fine, fairy-tale sheen and carrying the scent of coastal sage and ocean. It was going to be a damp day in Big Sur, at least through the morning. My partner and I were fluttering around the car, in the final stages of trip preparation, tightening pack straps and double-checking where we put the lighter.

"Ready to go?" I asked brightly.

"Yes!" he responded.

I rose from tightening my boot lace to find him hovering over me. A beat of silence passed. He stuck out a stick of deodorant and held it in the air between us.

"Do you, uh . . . do you think we should take this?"

I stared at the little blue tube.

One of the first backpacking lessons I remember being truly shocked by was that deodorant is anathema. "It has no function," my backpacking teacher Patchen had said. It was presented to us as a vestigial bauble of civilization, that is, the place we were walking away from. In the wilderness, at best, it's a toy that costs precious ounces. At worst, it's a chemically scented beacon for bugs and bears.

My partner knew that I'd been taught this. He knew I thought it was awkward, but that I'd chosen to follow this advice anyway, at least in the past. So he wasn't really asking, "Do you think we should take deodorant?" He was asking, "Do you think we are really ready to smell each other's BO on purpose?"

We'd been dating for a little over a year. It was a fair question. As far as relationship tests go, there's going to IKEA, getting lost on vacation, and engaging in vigorous exercise together for over seventy-two hours without any deodorant.

I knew people who backpacked with their romantic partners. This was something I'd wanted to do for a long time; I'd never had a boyfriend who wanted to backpack with me (for the record, this wasn't because of the deodorant issue, but "because it looks just like Skyrim, so why can't I just stay home"), and I was excited that we were about to go on our first trip. But there was a huge risk. We were going to see each other scruffy, puffy, unbrushed, and raw, in a traumatically honest and unsensual way. We'd talked about this, laughed about it, made a show of making peace with how nasty we were inevitably going to get with each other.

But, in that moment, that little stick of deodorant wasn't just deodorant. It was an offering to pretend that, in addition to the romance of the stars and the vistas and the sunrises, this other more uncomfortable reality wasn't going to come for us. That maybe we could still pretend a bit longer, for each other, that we were something other than human beings. For what is romance, if not to lovingly con someone into thinking you are anything but a sweating, shedding, panting primate with bacterial colonies living all over you? The deodorant was the fingers of romance, clinging to a branch over the black pit of reality. It was a bunch of roses. A diamond ring. A white flag asking, "What if we kept pretending just a little longer?"

I hated that he asked me, because I didn't want to be the one that said no. Who wants to insist to their partner on the right to smell bad? I love deodorant. At any given time, there are two sticks sitting in my room and one on my person. I have three kinds of leave-in hair gel and strong opinions about different perfume brands' interpretation of lilac. I love smelling good, and furthermore, I believe that love is both accepting your partner for who they are and also believing they are worth the time to make yourself lovely for. I didn't want to be the one to insist we had to stamp on romance's fingers and watch it fall into the darkness.

But it would be another seven ounces that we had to remember to chuck into the bear canister at night. At best, it was unnecessary. At worst, it was a liability. This was what Chuck and Patchen taught me.

I looked at my boyfriend. We locked eyes. I wanted him to see that I was afraid too. I chose my words very carefully: "I don't think we should take the extra weight."

I hope he could understand what I meant: "Goddammit, I love you. Your body doesn't scare me. I am not afraid of what you really are, under all the pretty trappings of society. And I hope you will in turn accept me."

Later I found out he chucked the deodorant in his pack without telling me. By day two, I smelled like a fermented onion and he smelled like wood spice. He thought this was hilarious. I stole all his MiO drops and told him they were lost. Miraculously at the time of writing we are still together.

YOUR PHYSICAL BODY—WHAT IT DOES and what it needs while you are miles away from a properly stocked bathroom—is a critical part of backpacking. Ironically, it's also a part I've found no one really wants to talk about in a practical manner. Probably because it's gross.

Backpacking is about returning to nature. That, unfortunately, includes embracing your natural self: unscented, unshaven, unshampooed . . . basically, something nobody would want to embrace. The iconic image of a modern backpacker is a clean-looking person standing on a cliff's edge and throwing their hands in the air, every ounce of their body screaming, "I have finally figured out the answer to every Zen riddle." Above all, the whole scene looks very fresh. We imagine it smells that way too. This is a lie.

Unfortunately, Instagram has given us the impression that three days out from the trailhead our hair can still be shiny, our nails clean, and our skin even-toned. Please let me shatter this illusion for you. Everyone on Instagram is lying. I know you think you know this; countless jokes and articles and memes remind us every day that the way people present themselves on social media is a sham and we shouldn't let it get under our skin, so to speak. But we continue to swipe and "like" and share and then turn off the screen and experience a flutter of panic as we catch a glimpse of ourselves in the mirror: are we as pretty, as interesting, and, ultimately, as good as the people we just saw?

We live in a visually focused society where looking good is incredibly important, possibly more so now than it's ever been in history. Taking meticulous care of your appearance isn't vanity—it's strategy. In our culture, being physically attractive gets you romantic partners, jobs, free stuff, and out of speeding tickets. This is true for all genders, but especially for women.

And here I am, asking you to knock it off. If you've never tried it before, this is somewhat radical stuff. Asking a woman to skip makeup, accept body odor, or deal with productless hair for an entire week—knowing there will be a camera around—is a bold proposition. It would be normal to respond to this suggestion with shrieking, terror, or even a light fainting spell (seriously). I'm not here to shame you for being afraid of looking ugly in a society that has taught you—*proven* to you—that beauty is a moneymaker.

But remember: We're not going to be in society anymore. Once you're out in the wilderness, all these fears will go away. Your desire to be beautiful and smell perfect at all times will diminish as a whole class of more important thoughts demand your mental attention. For example, obsessing over whether that tickling feeling in your shoe is in fact your bandage gently falling off or perhaps mentally undressing the paper from a hot, glistening cheeseburger. You'll barely notice if your hair has knots, your face has a zit, or the smell of your feet could stun a baby. The onslaught of offensively fresh air usually overpowers anything coming out of your armpits, anyway. It's weird, but eventually you learn the difference between "functionally clean" and "ceremoniously clean," and become comfortable aiming for the former—at least out here.

If the idea of leaving behind the zillions of beauty accoutrements you need to be taken seriously in the workplace is still too stressful, here's a tip: turn the camera away from you. That way no one will know what you looked like out there. If you do want to take some shots of yourself in the backcountry (because of course you do), just use filters on them when you get home. Filters are amazing! Don't be embarrassed. All your favorite bloggers and magazines and Instagramers are using them, and you can too. (You don't think anyone actually wakes up like that do you? And don't say Beyoncé—she isn't human; she's an immortal being made of light. Stop comparing yourself to her.)

But maybe it's not society that you want to be pretty for. Maybe you are hiking with a relatively new sweetie in an attempt to kindle bonding by forcing them to walk behind you and stare at your increasingly toned butt all day. Backpacking is a great strategy for accomplishing this goal, but there's a flip side. You're going to see parts of each other that are usually left hidden, unless you share a studio apartment, have jointly taken care of a newborn, or watched the other person get admitted to a hospital. Nothing tests a relationship like stumbling upon your boo taking a magnificent shit behind a tree, or smelling . . . whatever in god's name that is . . . when they take off their pants on night four in the humid confines of your shared

WHAT TO LEAVE AT HOME

Here's a list of common items I've had people ask me whether they should bring in their backcountry hygiene kit (all of which I've said no to):

1. **Deodorant.** Seriously. You're not gonna die without it; you're not gonna get an infection. The only person who can smell you is you. If you have companions, they'll be too distracted by their own monstrous self-scent discovery journey to bother judging yours. After the fascination of "is that really me?!" wears off, your nose basically becomes numb to it anyway. Just get through the first day. I promise you'll be fine.

2. **Shampoo and conditioner.** Yes, your hair is going to get greasy, but do not bring these things. They take up precious pack space, add unnecessary weight, and might make a bear mistake your scalp for a mango-coconut fruit platter.

3. **Razor.** Prepare to marvel with unbridled fascination as you watch your leg and armpit hair actually growing out. It's OK—you can shave it all off when you return to civilization. It can be our little secret you ever let it get this bad. (Men, most of you have known for years what you look like when you fail to shave, so enjoy the stifled sobs of your female compatriots as they discover themselves.)

4. **Hair dryer.** I know there are no dumb questions, but if you need me to tell you not to bring this, I'm worried about you.

tent. Backpacking together is definitely a test of how unconditional your love really is. Consider that before pitching it as a second date idea.

On the topic of backpacking with sweeties, let's address something I know a lot of you really want to hear about: sex. We all want to have ecstatic, bodice-ripping sex in a moonlit forest glade in the middle of nowhere. And while I hope all of you get to do that someday, backpacking is probably not the time for it. Why? If the idea of going to the gym for a whole day, not showering, and then coming home and giving your honey bedroom eyes makes you cringe, imagine adding dirt. If you're smart, you're thinking, "Condoms reduce bacterial transmissions, right?" Well, yes, but flinging a semen-filled latex balloon out of your tent in the middle of the night is the textbook opposite of Leave No Trace. Even if you don't mind packing out a used prophylactic in your waste bag (or you use a condomless form of birth control), there's a larger truth to contend with: mashing two sweat-crusted, unwashed meat packs together for ten to twenty minutes is basically an infomercial for a yeast infection.

I'm not saying don't do it. I'm just saying think it through.

WHAT TO PACK

So how does one keep their body functionally clean under a doctrine of ambitious minimalism? The following list is what I take in my backcountry beauty kit, and while I'm tempted to say it's what you should bring in yours, that would make me pretty egotistical. Consider this a helpful place to start, and modify as needed:

1. **The blessed bandana.** Wet it down, with or without a little biodegradable soap, and use it to rub and scrub anywhere you like. Then rinse it out (away from any natural body of water), and tie it on the back of your pack to dry. You can use it over and over again on any part of your body.

2. **Toothbrush and toothpaste.** Some ultralight seraphim among us might say don't bother. I say bother. I eat a lot of Swedish Fish when I backpack because sugar makes me happy, so oral care is pretty important to me. Toothbrushes can be super light, especially if you cut off part of the handle or bring the super tiny spare head of an electric toothbrush to use by itself. To cut further down on weight, carry baking soda or tooth cleaning powder instead of toothpaste (you can find it at health food stores or online).

3. **Salve.** Thick, buttery, creamy—the kind of thing you might mistake for Kerrygold butter in the middle of the night. If this is your first time walking with a heavy backpack for multiple days in a row, you're gonna be chafing and chapping in areas you didn't even know could chafe and chap. Wind and sun will blast your skin at far higher rates than it might be used to. In other words, your skin is going to fucking hate you. So, to apologize, get a thick, quick-absorbing salve that can be rubbed without question on every single part of your body. This stuff will be used for sunburns, friction burns, cooking

burns, dry hands, chapped lips, rashes, and a ton of other things you can't even imagine yet. I'm a big fan of anything shea butter or beeswax based. In fact, my personal favorite is a little container of 100 percent unscented shea butter. Carry this. Love this. This is your new favorite thing.

4. **Sunscreen.** I'm talking to everybody here, and I mean *everybody*. Whatever SPF or brand makes you happy. If you don't normally spend twelve hours a day under an open sky, especially an open sky at high elevation, you need sunscreen. Wear it on your neck, your ears, your elbows, the tops of your hands—all kinds of places you might not normally think of. Don't worry, whatever spots you miss on the first day the sun will find—nature's helpful reminder for the rest of your trip.

5. **Your most comfortable underwear.** This probably belongs in the clothing section, but the wrong undies can create so many hygienic problems that it's worth mentioning here. If things start to chafe around your underwear line, don't panic. Try changing your underwear, or even forgoing undies entirely (I promise, no matter what you're imagining, this is not as sexy as it sounds).

6. **Tampons or a menstrual cup, if applicable.** (More on this in the next section.)

7. **Biodegradable soap.** Campsuds is an old favorite of mine, and travel-size bottles of concentrated Dr. Bronner's are also great (the love sermons on the labels double as fantastic backcountry bathroom reading material). Whatever soap you pick, just ensure it's unscented and biodegradable. Seriously. I'm trusting you. The streams, rivers, lakes, and ponds of the wild are all in your care—and at your mercy—when you visit them. It is not very nice or neighborly to visit a pristine mountain river, enjoy its bounty, and then leave it laced with the signature scent of your favorite Sugar Peach Frappé Body Wash. The fish will not be impressed. The trees will be furious. Princess Mononoke will come at your tent with an axe in the night. Keep your soap as unscented and earth friendly as possible.

8. **Hand sanitizer.** A little rubdown after you use the backcountry restroom is a considerate thing to do, both for your friends and for your health.

9. **Baby wipes.** This is an optional luxury in which I regularly indulge. Baby wipes are a little heavy because they are soaked in liquid and, like everything else, must be packed out. But you'll be astounded at how quickly two squares of damp cloth can feel like an entire shower. Aim for fragrance-free to avoid attracting bugs. Plus, fragrance-free wipes are typically gentler on your skin.

A little baby wipe here, a little salve there, some clean undies, and you're practically Cinderella. And that's it. That's your whole toilette. I'm so excited. You're gonna be so pretty.

HOW TO WASH YOURSELF OUTSIDE

In my experience, Leave No Trace principles are the hardest to stick to when it comes to personal hygiene: you must take any of your human run-off—whether culinary, cleansing, or caca—and bury it at least two hundred feet away from any major body of water. That includes soap. Yes, even if the soap comes in a bottle plastered with a hippie's love sermon that swears it's more earth friendly than a vegan dreamcatcher. Preservatives and foaming agents can encourage algae blooms and generally throw off the microbial balance in the water. No, not your tiny drops of soap specifically, but everyone's tiny drops add up to very big concentrations. So we all must do our part.

Instead of bathing directly in a lake or river, LNT principles dictate that you must scoop up some water, carry it more than two hundred feet from its source, and bathe there. This "take a shower two hundred feet away from the flowing water" advice is repeated all over the internet, on multiple blogs and how-to articles. But I have never heard the technical details of how it's done. I guess you lather yourself up in soap and then pour water bottles over your head until all the soap is on the ground, and then you're naked and wet in the middle of the jungle and this is considered success. It might honestly work if the weather is hot and there's no one else around

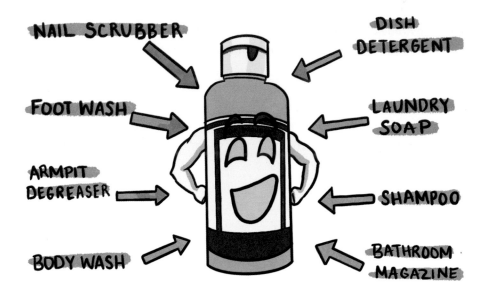

to gawk at you. But if it's cold or you're on a crowded trail, this advice is insulting. I don't know why so many outdoor enthusiasts keep repeating it, because I don't think anyone is actually doing it.

I do my best to follow Leave No Trace, so I typically stay clean in the great outdoors by wading into the water and scrubbing down with a bandana without any soap at all, or spot cleaning on dry land with a baby wipe. You can get a surprising amount of odor and dirt off your body with simple elbow grease, water, and a bandana. The bandana is really key.

Imagine you have been hiking for four hours uphill. Your eyes are tearing from the salty sweat running into them. Your body odor is out of control. You are overheated, beet-red, and want to yell "fuck everything that ever existed." Then you crest a hill. A glittering lake appears, as wide and deep as the sky, nestled beneath towers of granite, shielding you from the unforgiving sun. You say a prayer to the gods of bathtime and fling yourself with careless abandon into this divine temple. It's amazing. But when you get out, that baptized feeling quickly vanishes. Soon you realize swimming around like a mystical mountain mermaid doesn't actually make you as clean as one. It'll wash the sweat off, but without friction you're still covered in almost as much human dirt and BO as before. This is where the bandana comes in: you gotta get in there and really rub down. Otherwise you'll emerge from the water the same onion-flavored mountain orc you were an hour ago—just a wet one now.

If you have a cut or scrape, however, it's pretty important to wash it once a day with both soap and water. Even the superficial ouchies you would completely ignore at home. I have a coin-sized scar on my knee, from a fungal infection when I was sixteen that grew out of a pin-sized ingrown hair I simply forgot to wash in the backcountry. (Oh, don't make that face. How often do you remember to sit down and methodically wash your knees?).

Biodegradable soap is also helpful for washing your hair. Using a harsh, oil-cutting soap is verboten in my pampered-curl hair care routine at home, but in the backcountry, it's time for the big guns. When your scalp starts to feel like a hot, greasy sponge after days of hiking and sweating, give yourself a little spa treatment. Flip your head upside down, grab your water bottle, and pour out just enough water to wet your scalp. Squeeze a small amount of soap onto your fingertips (less is best with these backcountry soap concentrates) and, working back to front, give yourself a delicious scalp massage. When you're done, pour the rest of the water bottle on your hair to rinse.

Voila. You've washed your hair with the kind of water conservancy that would make the CEO of Greenpeace jealous, surrounded by the sounds of nature, flowers, and scenic vistas. This is a scenario many spas charge $300 to recreate. And you're doing it with a Nalgene and two cents' worth of Dr. Bronner's. Way to stick it to the beauty industry.

Every now and again you may want a little more cleaning power than simple water and friction can provide, but maybe you don't feel like standing out in the open naked—pouring water bottles on your head. This is where baby wipes shine. Take out a baby wipe or two, and rub down the areas that need it most (usually naughty bits, armpits, or feet). Be sure to use a separate wipe for each census-designated bacterial zone. You don't want the guys on your feet swapping ideas with the guys on your junk. The downside to baby wipes is that they must be packed out, so using six a day can add up to an anxiety-inducing amount of weight. However, using one or two a day (especially after going to the bathroom) is a really great way to feel fresh as a daisy.

A final, fun option is to use ashes as soap. This is a neat trick I learned from reading Dave Canterbury's *Bushcraft 101* while wondering why he was so much cooler than me. The trouble is, I don't usually make big, delicious, ashy campfires when I backpack, as fires are generally not allowed on the West Coast. However, if you find yourself tramping through a place that allows the kind of big, beautiful fires that most Californians associate with billion-dollar settlements—good news! Some ash, a wet hanky, and you've got yourself a proper bath. If you're brave, you can even use the ashes as toothpaste. Thanks, Dave.

HOW TO HIKE WITH A VAGINA

I'd like to make a confession. Being a cis woman in the wilderness sucks. I know I'm going to get a lot of hate mail for that, but there, I said it. Yes, women (all women) belong outside. Yes, women are strong enough, smart enough, and worthy enough. Yes, I encourage all women to backpack, and to flip the bird to literally anyone who tells us that we can't. But I'm also going to tell you that you'll never get penis envy like when you hear someone unzip their tent flap at three in the morning on a snowy night to take a whiz, *while the rest of their body stays warm inside the fucking tent.*

Meanwhile, to perform the same activity with a vagina, you have to clamber out of your sleeping bag, fumble with your boots while whispering "sorry, sorry" for scalding your tent-mate's eyes with your headlamp, then throw your body outside, feel the cold bitchslap your face, beeline for the heart of a forest that looks like a scene from *The Blair Witch Project*, and when you get to the edge, rip off your pants, squat down, and present your entire pubic buffet to ALL the sharp-toothed demons who live there.

I can't say I love this.

Furthermore, we usually can't hike with our shirts off when it's hot. And our friends, parents, and lovers often helpfully wonder aloud if we are more likely to be eaten alive because we leak fluid that attracts apex predators, even though this has been debunked. We are also used to city statistics that say we are more likely to be rape and murder targets (especially if you're a trans woman). This is the reality of being a woman outside.

But most of us have been dealing with a "reality" that is full of assholes, creeps, infantilizers, and abrupt, red messes since we were in middle school, right? Give yourself some credit. You figured it out then, and you can figure it out now.

Menstruation while backpacking is a pain in the ass. There are many schools of thought as to how to deal with it. Let's talk about the options:

1. Don't. Use a type of birth control that delays or prevents your period from occurring or plan your trip for a time when you won't be having your period.
2. Use pads. (Don't do this. It's a joke. I wrote this as a joke.)
3. Use tampons. Applicator-free tampons aren't a bad idea, as they can cut down on weight and paper waste. But remember you have to pack these out (YES, you do).
4. Get a menstrual cup. These were basically designed for backpacking, and you'll hear many backpackers extol them. If you can use one, do it.

I know I'm supposed to say something like "all of these options are equal, you're a moon goddess and whatever you choose to put in or near your yoni is perfect." But I can't sit here and pretend that some of these options aren't better than others. Pads would be ridiculously bulky to carry both into and out of the wilderness, and they increase your risk of developing clinical swamp ass. They're not just inconvenient; they might actually be harmful.

Tampons are OK, but even without applicators they still take up some pack space. The worst part about tampons is that you have to pack them out. To top it off, you'll have to pop that hot little bag in your bear canister every night.

You might be thinking, "That's disgusting. Why can't I just bury my used tampons? They're organic, or whatever, right?" Not really. Even the purest, high-brow, biodegradable cotton tampons take six months to break down. The normal, cheap kind, typically a mix of rayon and cotton, will take years longer. If you don't care about LNT, also know that many curious critters will dig them up and scatter them around, and other backpackers will see them. Frankly, it's rude. We're backpackers, not barbarians. Get it together.

In my humble opinion, if your body is willing to work with a menstrual cup, do it. Just give yourself a few months' practice before your first trip (do not, I repeat, do not make the backcountry the place where you learn to use a menstrual cup).

Menstrual cups last a long time, take up less space in your pack than a bunch of bulky cotton, and you don't have to pack out anything other than the little lightweight half-ounce cup itself. You can also leave it in for twelve hours, which means you only have to take it out twice a day. Simply go a few hundred feet away from any rivers, lakes, or camps, dig a hole, sanitize your hands, take the cup out, bury your business, rinse the cup and your hands with some clean, filtered water, reinsert, and, finally, rub your hands down with some sanitizer again. You can take the opportunity to rinse your bits as well. That's it. This is unfathomably easier than the alternatives.

One last bit of period advice: travel, stress, and changes in your sleep schedule can affect your cycle. There's a chance you'll get a weird surprise in your undies even if you aren't expecting it. Similarly, if your period doesn't come on time after your trip, don't panic. You did not get impregnated by an elk and then forget about it. Of course, see a professional if you're worried about changes to your cycle, but know that changes in your period schedule are pretty common after bursts of high activity and travel, and there's a good chance nothing is wrong at all.

Besides your period, you may also be wondering about yeast infections in the wild. A lot of people, not insanely, have a mild flutter of panic at the thought of what exercising for multiple days in a row without a shower might do to the notoriously sensitive balance of flora between their legs. Every honeypot is unique and reacts differently to changes in its routine. I have talked to many people about this, and the feedback I've gotten is as wild and variable as . . . well . . . vaginas. So I'm not going to pretend to know how your business will to react to the wilderness. You're going to have to apply some "know thyself" logic here. What I can do instead is offer you the same contradictory, confusing advice that has been given to me:

1. Wear cotton undies.
2. Don't let anyone tell you what to put in your vagina.
3. Avoid baby wipes . . . or don't.

I know I went on a whole rant earlier about how cotton kills, but this is the one area where, ironically, cotton saves. I rarely say "should" in this book, but I'd like to say it now: you should only wear cotton, wool-blend, or bamboo underwear when you backpack. This is because these fabrics breathe, and undies made out of these materials are thin enough that they'll dry quickly. This is what you want against this part of your body. It's also a good idea to change your undies once a day.

I did not interview many swamp ass scientists at the Swamp Ass Institute of Swampology for this book, but in my personal experience, using an unscented baby wipe on your junk once a day helps keep things relatively clean (scented baby wipes can cause irritation for a lot of people, especially in such a sensitive area). But if you don't react well to the chemicals in baby wipes, even the fragrance-free ones, don't start using them in the backcountry. I've heard from many people that a rinse of the undercarriage with clean, filtered water helps immensely. This applies to all genders. Just squat under a stream from your water bottle for a refreshing backcountry bidet.

You don't need to use soap on your privates every day—in fact, according to a number of people who are much more qualified than I am, using too much soap downstairs can cause more problems than it solves. Just rinse, change out of wet undies before bed, and always, always, always wipe from front to back. If you start to feel irritation, try sleeping or hiking without any underwear (to make things extra breathable).

The vagina is a remarkable organ, capable of taking a ton of abuse. It tends to take care of itself if you get out of its way. However, if you know you are susceptible to yeast infections, are going on a trip where you suspect your pants will be wet most or all of the time (see: river rafting), or just can't handle the fear, pack a packet of Monistat as part of your med kit. There's a chance you won't need it, but there's also a chance you'll be someone's hero.

HOW TO HIKE WITH A PENIS
This is just a guess:

1. Enjoy it.
2. Maybe . . . like . . . wash it sometimes.

Chapter 10

POOP
Yes, It Deserves Its
Own Chapter

"Don't squat in high grass. I shit on myself once trying to do that."
   —A backpacking expert

It was September, three weeks into my year at Team, the alternative high school where I was learning about wilderness medicine and backpacking in addition to math, English, and history. My eyes were fixed on our grizzled teacher, Chuck, as he prepped a demonstration at the front of the classroom. He was moving his mouth, but I couldn't really hear him. He paused his lecture to present exhibit A: his index finger, covered in gel, moving in a come-hither motion toward us while his eyebrows wiggled up and down. I and the twenty-three other teenagers in the room began to mewl in anguish, diving into our sweatshirts with shudders and gags.

This was my first proper lecture about shitting in the wilderness. We were one week away from our first backpacking trip, which would take place in California's Sierra Nevada. At roughly twelve days, it would be the longest backpacking trip I'd ever taken. Most of my classmates had never been on more than a day hike, so this was going to be a lot of people's first time going number two in the woods. Including me. Chuck was stressing the significance of proper hygiene protocols for this expedition, but he was also addressing the elephant in the room: our fear of taking a dookie outside. Ours were pampered upper-middle-class American butts. And American butts are addicted to toilet seats.

He told us, "I know some of you are scared of going poop without a toilet. Some of you might not want to. Some of you might try to hold it, because you're so afraid. Well, if you do that, your fecal matter will become impacted. It will harden in your colon. It could rupture. I am responsible for your well-being out there. So, if you don't go, this is what I'll have to do to get it out."

He wiggled his finger again. We all but screamed.

Two weeks later, when I felt my bowels stir on my first morning in the Sierra, I felt no hesitation in marching off to take my first ever shit in the woods. All my fear was gone. Nothing is scarier than the idea of giving your teacher a medical mandate to stick a finger up your ass.

WHY DID I DEDICATE AN entire chapter to defecation? Why can't I lean into the fact that you're an adult, and one of the classic and oft-cited hallmarks of adulthood is the ability to wipe your own ass? Well, because when you take a potty-trained human and throw them into the wild, not everything comes naturally. Furthermore, walking a lot more than you usually do, in conditions you aren't used to, can complicate things downstairs (the technical term for the condition is "swamp ass" or "monkey butt"). I'm not gonna presume to know how you currently handle your downstairs post-bowel movement, but if you skip this chapter and end up with diaper rash or a fungal infection as a full-fledged adult, at least I'll know I tried.

There is something simultaneously scary and freeing about pooping in the woods. Defecation is probably the most private thing you do on a regular basis at home (one assumes). Now, far away from all the tools you use to deal with it in a clean, secret, and quintessentially civilized manner, you are going to poop under an open sky, the definition of a wild animal. It's going to feel very different. Vulnerable. You might find yourself averse to the idea—afraid even—but have faith.

Many people find squatting to be easier than sitting on their toilet at home, as it helps the rectal muscles move. In fact, many, many people around the world still relieve themselves simply by squatting and aiming. Humanity has been shitting in holes for far longer than we've been shitting in toilets. Regardless, if you're like me, and you grew up in a society that trained kids to go straight from diapers to porcelain, don't worry. The learning curve is fast. Welcome back to the ground, my friend.

ASSEMBLING YOUR SHIT KIT

First, let's talk about your materials. Most backcountry backpacks have a little zippered pouch on the underside of the brain, or topmost lid. It looks like it would be a good place to hide identity forging documents or cash from the mafia, but in fact this discreet, easily accessible pocket is designed for storing your "poo caddy."

I recommend you include the following:

1. **Hand sanitizer.** Since you won't have a sink to wash your hands in the wilderness, and consequences are rather high if you have an accident with the toilet paper, this stuff is a really great idea. A little travel-size bottle should do.
2. **Toilet paper.** As much as you think you'll need for the duration of your trip (and then maybe a little more for insurance). Store it in a clear ziplock bag (even if you are planning to smash half a roll into your pack) when you suspect any precipitation may occur.
3. **A gallon ziplock bag.** Cover it in duct tape or mark it with something that indicates danger, like big, red cartoon *X*s or a picture of Harvey Weinstein. Put yet another ziplock bag inside this bag.
4. **A bidet bottle.** Another option is a bidet cap to put on a soft bodied water bottle. (Optional)
5. **Baby wipes.** (Optional)
6. **A little orange shovel.** So you can dig a grave for your turds.

ASSESSING YOUR FITNESS FOR OUTDOOR DEFECATION

We all have different strengths and weaknesses. For example, you might be the roughest, rippest guy in town. But maybe you haven't done a butterfly stretch since you were in preschool, or you have a knee injury that never fully healed. Figuring out if you can squat, while being comfortable enough to relax your bowels is important to ascertain *before* there are no toilets around. So go ahead and try it now.

Put this riveting book down, stand up, spread your legs nice and wide, and waddle into a squat. Aim your knees such that they track right over your big toe as you go down. How do you feel? Are you stable? Are your knees screaming? Could you relax here for a minute?

If the squat isn't working out, it's OK. Really! It's OK. When you're out there, using brown-vision to scope out a place to deposit your waste, you'll find that Mother Nature often provides a big rock to lean against or a tree that you can grab onto. Some people even just sit on a log, after digging a hole behind it. You'll have to prep your area a little more, but everything else works the same.

FINDING A PLACE TO POOP

Regardless of whether you use your own body weight or employ the help of a rock or tree, here are some general rules about where to go number two outside:

1. **Scout.** Make sure you're at least two hundred feet from any lake or stream, in keeping with Leave No Trace practices. This is how we avoid drinking each other's shit particulates. Shitting in someone else's water is very impolite. Don't do it.
2. **Dig.** Your hole should be around six to eight inches deep. This is where Mr. Orange Shovel comes in. If you want, you can leave the shovel at home and use your hands or a rock to dig, but most backpackers find the shovel makes things easier, cleaner, and faster.
3. **Squat.** Trust.
4. **Cleanse.** If you feel the need, use a baby wipe or a bit of water to rinse yourself. A bidet bottle—a portable, soft-bodied plastic bottle with a spray nose designed explicitly for aiming at your nethers—is great for this. If you're feeling decadent, and have ounces to spare, this is a lovely thing to bring along.[39]

   Alternately, if your aim is killer, you can use your regular water bottle to rinse yourself off. Whichever system you choose, be sure to use filtered water, and always aim front to back. You don't have to cleanse every time, but most backpackers find it the ideal prophylactic for swamp ass.

---

39. You can also make your own bidet bottle from a soft-plastic, disposable water bottle with a hole punched in the lid. See YouTube for instructions.

5. **Wipe.** Use that toilet paper you responsibly stocked in a ziplock bag to remove any excess moisture. Some bidet-bottle users find that in certain environments, things air dry without the need for additional toilet paper.

   But if you choose to wipe, there is a bit of a method to it. Wipe once, observe, and then fold the paper in half and wipe again. Do this (swapping in new squares once your folds become origami masterpieces) until there is nothing—nothing—left on the paper. This method gets you more than one wipe out of a stretch of paper, so that you can pack less and still have more paper than you need.

6. **Conceal.** Take the soiled wipes and/or toilet paper and put them into the ziplock bag inside of the ziplock that has the picture of Harvey Weinstein's face on it. Ensure that both bags are zipped close. Reminder: we're talking about toilet paper soaked in your own shit, so let's really focus on those zips.

7. **Cover.** Bury your shame.

8. **Sanitize.** Give your hands a nice little bath with that sanitizer.

9. **Leave.** Carry on your merry way.

ASKING YOURSELF, "CAN I PUT THAT ON MY BUTTCRACK?"

I have read a few books that suggest a rock or a leaf is a perfectly sufficient substitute for toilet paper. I think this advice should be reserved specifically for seasoned, ambitious campers with strong buttholes. But even an amateur like me can see the appeal of the argument: "Why carry toilet paper all the way out here? It's not like Caveman Bill had Charmin." Keenly observed, my minimalist friend. And I cannot say, despite having studied primate evolution at one of the world's top anthropological universities, that I know what Caveman Bill used to wipe his ass.

Instead, I would assert that the idea of using a rock to wipe sounds terrible. That's it, that's my only counterargument, but I feel pretty good about it, honestly. Perhaps I'm outing myself as a neat freak when I tell you I find the idea alarming because whatever residue is on the rocks will get on your bum.

A leaf might work, since it is a smoother surface and is perhaps easier to wipe clean on your pants before it is used to wipe your behind. However,

THE PEE RAG

You've probably seen a few female hikers with a paisley bandana tied to the outside of their pack. So #bohemian, right? Guess what, it's covered in pee.

If you're an American with a vagina, you probably wipe with toilet paper every time you go number one. You should still wipe in the backcountry, but there's no need to spend your toilet paper ration on this. Instead, many hikers opt to use something called a "pee rag": a cotton bandana you dedicate exclusively to the purpose of wiping your front lawn, and then tie to your backpack to dry. If upon reading that last sentence you are gagging uncontrollably and/or muttering "she better not be about to give me that 'urine is sterile' crap," don't worry, I'm not. I think urine is disgusting too.

To compensate for this, all backpackers have unanimously agreed that sunlight sterilizes things. It's not totally fake science. Marie Kondo says she dries her dishes outside on her porch because the sunlight sterilizes them. You don't hate sparks of joy, do you? No. But even before Kondo was widely known, backpackers believed in the sun's powers of sterilization as fervently as if they were carved onto the tablets of the Ten Commandments.

I don't really understand how such a group of relatively resourceful and intelligent people decided that sunbeams sterilize a urine-soaked rag, but still insist that you must use hand sanitizer after pooping instead of holding your palms to the sky like a faith healer, but I'd encourage you to not ask too many questions.

I've heard too many stories about people wiping their butts with poison oak. Even though I'm confident I could identify that glossy bastard in my sleep, I'm too afraid that one day, overconfident and overtrusting in an unfamiliar environment, I will incorrectly identify some new flora, use it to wipe, and then spend the rest of the day with an energetic allergic reaction in my butthole. Some experiences you don't even need to have once, you know?

I know not everyone in the world uses toilet paper, but they use something cleaner than leaves and rocks. It's a global constant, a human truth. Some cultures do it with their left hand, then meticulously wash that left hand, and do nothing else with it. But since there aren't any sinks out in the backcountry, this has never really appealed to me. Most Americans have been using toilet paper for as long as they can remember. If you've been using nothing else since you were potty trained, don't feel like you have to suddenly forgo toilet paper in addition to toilet seats.

However, if you're going someplace where you are quite familiar with the flora, and know welcoming, soft leaves will be plentiful, honestly, you don't have to be as paranoid as me. Just know there's no shame in using toilet paper. There are moments in backpacking when you want to prove you're a badass, and moments when you want to be comfortable. Ask yourself whom you're going to brag to about wiping your ass with a rock.

BURYING YOUR TOILET PAPER VS. PACKING OUT

Back in Team, I was taught to pack out all used toilet paper and related waste, including wipes, waste paper, and menstrual products. Burying them wasn't up for debate. Granted, this mandate came from men who threatened to anally probe us if we expressed too much cowardice at shitting outside, but still.

I want to address the elephant in the room that this entire concept is gross, without pretending it is Draconian. It simply adheres to Leave No Trace principles. I also want to address the other elephant in the room, the one representing the school of thought that claims that as long as you bury your toilet paper in a deep cathole you don't have to pack it out. Then, I want to invite both elephants to go hiking with me to scenic vistas and on family-friendly trails in the most popular parks, and observe the little toilet paper blooms that litter the ground. Tangled in bushes, rolling like tumbleweed—look, that one looks like a nuclear reactive dandelion floating through the air. It doesn't seem to matter whether park rules dictate that visitors must pack out used toilet paper, or if it's permissible to bury it in a cathole. What seems to matter is whether a lot of people visit a particular place.

Nothing interrupts your fantasy of pretending to be Aragorn on your way to rescue the Hobbits from Isengard more than stumbling onto someone else's shit-covered paper, paper they ran away from because they thought it was gross. Considering how many people are venturing out of their connected homes to reconnect with the pristine vastness of nature, and also how many wild animals consider it a fun Saturday night trivia competition to dig up buried TP and guess what you ate, my personal philosophy is to pack it out. But that's just me. You don't have to. I hear the ninth circle of hell isn't so bad.

SHITTING IN A BAG

In some circumstances, such as in the snow or on a glacier, you are not allowed to defecate on the ground. This is because, instead of biodegrading, your poop will just kind of freeze there, like a big shitsicle. Other people will see it when they walk by and think, "Gee, someone took a shit here."

If you're going to a place where you can't bury your shit, the ranger station or land manager in charge of the wilderness area will inform you of this pleasant fact, usually when issuing you a permit. They will suggest—no, *insist*—that you shit in a bag instead.

"Wag bags" or "blue bags," as they are often called, are usually required above tree line in popular national parks, such as Mount Whitney in California's Sequoia National Park or on Mauna Loa in Hawai'i Volcanoes National Park—places so beautiful, you will actually shit in a bag just to see them.

The bag has a lot of components, including a sheet of paper with a bull's-eye target, an inner bag, and some kitty litter. The idea is to take the paper out, aim at it, then wrap up your business in the paper, put it in the inner bag with the kitty litter, and, finally, put that bag in the bag everything came in. You then carry it with you. In your pack. The whole time.

The system does seem secure, and I don't know of anyone who has ever had an accident, but I can't blame people for feeling like this is a disaster waiting to happen. There are many worse things that can happen to you in the wilderness than poop, however.

For example, death.

Chapter 11

CRISIS
How to Act Natural When You're Pretty Sure You're About to Die

"My wilderness first-aid kit is just one of those tinfoil blankets and a bottle of Percocet. What is a Band-Aid going to do if I break my femur?"
—A backpacking expert

I grew up in the fog. More specifically, I grew up at the base of a mountain just north of San Francisco, a city so in love with its notorious weather pattern that they named it Karl. I learned to drive along cold, blustery cliffs wreathed in clouds as thick as pea soup, which obscured my windshield and reflected my car's headlights back in my face. Everyone I knew had hit a deer by age eighteen. So when I tell you about the time I was hiking in Chile, and I say, "It was too foggy to see in front of us," I am, for once, not being hyperbolic.

I was hiking on the cliffside of a volcano called Puyehue, in northern Patagonia. Jeanne had organized the trip with her friend Irina, a Chilean expat living in Germany. We probably wouldn't have known this volcano existed if not for Irina, as it's not a common hiking spot. In fact, we only saw one other person the entire time we were there. It was the motherlode of backpacking: tremendous natural splendor, all to ourselves.

On the first day, we hiked sheer up through a green, balmy forest for about eight hours straight. Teetering between our hiking poles and covered in sweat, we hit the edge of the tree line just as the sun fell behind the horizon. After sleeping in a hiker shelter, the next morning rewarded us with an unbounded blue sky presiding over an undulating planet made entirely of white pebbles. In the far distance, a mass of obsidian the size of a glacier curled at the tree line, and above us the towering top of the volcano, frosted in snow, watched our every move. Clouds were born and sizzled out of existence all around us. We were in the sky. We felt like gods.

The scree, although lovely in a kind of stark, Martian way, made an actual trail impossible—footprints and impressions don't last on a sea of tiny rocks the way they do on dirt, or even sand. The acute tilt of the volcano's cone and the expanse of the space also made it difficult to walk straight. To help hikers, the park service had installed poles around the rim of the volcano cone to serve as trail markers as you circumnavigated it. If in doubt, you could simply hike from one pole to the next, and know that you were on the right track.

This was what Jeanne, Irina, and I were doing. We'd hike to one pole, have a moment, cry about how beautiful everything was, and then walk on until we found the next one in the distance. Wash, rinse, and repeat. The poles started getting farther and farther apart, however. Eventually, we hadn't seen one in what felt like an incorrect amount of time, but it is hard to worry when you are floating above the world, impossible to feel lost when you can simply look down and see everything from above.

When the fog started to roll in, it was beautiful. Mountain air made into a soft, woolen blanket. It rushed up the side of the mountain like a tide coming in, over the tree line . . . up the cone . . . up to us. This can happen very fast on mountains, as if someone pressed fast-forward on a nature documentary, but you stayed in real time.

Undeterred by a little moisture, we kept walking until we realized that, yes, we definitely should have seen the next pole by now. We didn't know if we had moved up or down from the invisible line that connected the poles around the rim, but it was nowhere to be found. The fog was a chameleon, blending in with the gray and white rocks under our feet. Finally, realizing we had no idea where we were going or if we were even headed in a straight line anymore, we simply stopped walking. We were ants in a fog machine. We were blind.

"We could wait it out," I suggested.

"That could be all night," said Irina.

"We can't camp on this grade—it's too steep," said Jeanne.

We debated our options inside the cloud of fog. Finally, we opted to try to find the next pole using the one tool we had: each other. Irina went first, walking forward into the fog until Jeanne and I cried "stop!" just before we lost sight of her. Then I walked forward, past Jeanne, past Irina, gently crunching one foot in front of the other inside the muffled cloud, until I heard Irina say "stop," meaning I was about to leave her sight. There were probably no more than twenty paces between the three of us in this daisy chain, total. The poles were half a mile apart. Still, I peered forward into the mist, willing the red-tipped stick to appear, to tell me everything was fine, that everything was still going according to plan. That we weren't the word that was getting harder and harder to block from my mind: lost.

Turns out fog reflects not only headlights back into your face, but also hope. We repeated this scouting exercise a few more times, going a little up, then a little down, thinking maybe we were just out of line with the poles. Surely the next pole had to be there. But there was nothing.

I walked back to Irina and together we walked back to Jeanne. We sat in the pebbles, three lost frogs in a pond of gray. One of us pulled out the map, which had always held answers. We knew which way was down because of the slope of the volcano cone we were sitting on, but that was about all we could know. A map is only good if you can see.

"We should walk down," said Jeanne.

"Are you insane? We can't leave the trail," I said.

"We can't leave a trail we aren't even sure we're on anymore," she countered. "The last pole was an hour ago. We should have seen another one before the fog even came in."

"But we don't know what's down there, or if we can even walk it."

"We know there's water, and probably another trail, here, off to the east," said Jeanne, pointing at the map.

We were silent for a minute. That we couldn't stay here was obvious, but leaving the trail felt like walking out of a foggy frying pan into a fog fire.

Irina broke the tie. "We don't know when this will clear. It could be here all night. And we can't make camp—it's too steep."

I had been lost only once before in my life, while hiking in Redwood National Park. After leaving the trail to pee behind some nearby bushes, I ended up lost for fifteen minutes as I tried to find my way back to the clear, obvious trail that I could have sworn was right behind me. I'd say this is an indicator of my supreme unfitness for backcountry travel, but I know too many backpackers far more hardcore than me who have done the exact same thing. It really can happen that fast. A backcountry trail is basically an encouraging babysitter—one you never appreciate until they're gone—holding your hand thanklessly while Mother Nature threatens you on all sides. Letting go of that hand on accident is terrifying. Letting go on purpose feels like lunacy.

That's how I felt the entire time we walked down the volcano. The fog swirled between and around us, three ghosts trying to wander back into existence. Finally, after about thirty minutes, we broke through the fog line. In this new landscape, the rocks appeared to have been swept into hills and valleys, and the obsidian glacier in the distance was ever so slightly closer, with a now-visible ribbon of water winding down out of it. Behind us was the Nothing. In front of us were endless, frozen waves of scree. And not a trail in sight.

"Water is the most important thing," I heard a voice in my head say, a million years ago in another world, where I was safe in a kitchen making stir-fry. My mother.

I felt my heartbeat in my ears, a metal drum, thumping. My stomach was a pit of fire, and my blood had been replaced by an electric current that needed to be grounded in something familiar. I thought about my mother again. I saw my sisters' faces. Visions of a marriage I'd never had, a book deal I hadn't acquired . . . everything I hadn't done yet in life flashed before my eyes. My esophagus rose. I willed myself not to cry.

I turned to Jeanne. "We're lost, aren't we?"

She rolled her eyes in that way friends do when they have known each other for so long they can tell when the other is full of shit. "Diana, why do you always assume we are about to die?"

We hiked for a few more hours, splitting up and heading in different directions, but always remaining within sight of one another. We thought there might be a road or trail—not the one we wanted, but after a few hours of not knowing where you are, you'll kind of take anything.

Then another bank of fog began to form, curling and roiling down at the tree line. It paced back and forth and bounced, like a runner warming up at the starting line. I was far off from Irina and Jeanne, peering over a hill, trying to will a trail to the east into existence, when I realized the fog had snapped up from its starting line at the trees below. It was moving in, fast.

I looked back at my friends standing a few hills away to the west. They were looking pointedly in my direction and waving their arms. My lizard brain did the algebra on the speed of the fog running toward me and the speed of me running west, back to them and my pack, my clothing, my water, my flashlight, everything, before issuing a verdict: *run*.

I tore down the hill, sliding down the scree and then bolting up the other side, running as fast as my muscles could respond. I'd like to tell you I was thinking something cheeky and self-deprecating at the time, like "Why do you eat so much cake, Diana?" or "Why didn't you take CrossFit, Diana?" but the truth is I was too scared. My lungs burned as my heart burst into its red zone bpms. I didn't know I could run that fast. Just as the fog began to overtake me, I grabbed their hands. Then it closed in again, washing out everything and drowning us in silence. We were back inside the Nothing. This time with the added seasoning of having tried to find a trail, and failed.

Since the sun was setting, and we couldn't see anyway, we decided to camp right where we were. It was flat enough. We had enough water to get through the night.

We pitched our tent quietly, dutifully setting up our cooking area and zipping our jackets up to our chins. I savored the motions of plugging the fuel canister into the stove and stirring something warm inside a pot: familiar steps with reliable outcomes, predictable things we could still do for ourselves. There was no wood to burn above the tree line; there were just rocks and sky. But we sat in a circle as if there was a fire between us anyway, not speaking. Irina had her hands folded in her lap. Jeanne was stirring the cookpot. I was simply trying not to speak, because I was too afraid that nothing would come out but the blubbering fears of a lost girl who was really regretting never finishing Tom Brown's field guides.

The light faded like a bird diving into an ocean—then we were in deep darkness. I thought about the cell phone in my pack. There was a comfort. I could use it to call for help if I needed to, couldn't I? Wait, was there service up here? No, certainly not, but probably emergency service, right? How much would that cost? Would my GPS work? I'd never needed to be evacuated before. When would I know it was the right time to ask for rescue? My thoughts swam in and out of my head with the fog, dragging me down into a pit of guilt, shame, and fear.

Then, after an hour, the fog left. Fast again, like someone had come along with a push broom and simply whooshed it out of the way. Suddenly, a light was on above us. I looked up and had to look away again, the moon was so bright. I blinked into the brightness, my eyes growing wide into a landscape of moonbeams. White hill crests twirled in all directions and our shadows leaned behind us, as clear as on a summer's day. We could see over a mile away, but there was nothing to see except the hills, the dark sky, and the alien sun. It was the most beautiful thing I had ever seen.

I again gazed up into this divine nightlight, spellbound, my eyes adjusting. Night did not have to mean darkness. I suddenly realized why every single language on earth had multiple ways to name a newborn child "moon."

I began to sing.

"Moon is shining, the weather is sweet, yeah."

Jeanne and Irina looked at me.

"Make you wanna move, your hiking feet now . . . "

Jeanne blinked.

"Oh, to the rescue," I continued. "No one . . . comes . . . ?"

I looked back at them.

"OH NO NO NO NO NO," I cried into the scree, and the three of us exploded, laughing, mad with the need for joy. We howled under the moon, into the ghost-white world, screaming, our eyes filling with tears.

THE TITLE OF THIS BOOK was originally going to be "Jeanne and Diana's Guide to Backcountry Dancing," and it was going to be a list of nonsensical dance steps you could execute upon reaching the point in a backpacking journey where insanity sets in—usually around day three or four, before anyone has been seriously hurt, but after at least one person has fallen into a river, had their pack straps chewed off by a mouse, or ripped open the seat of their pants on a rock. You realize you cannot win and you have no control over anything out here (you never did), and either the sheer relief or sheer terror of that realization induces a kind of madness. This madness is almost always expressed as uncontrollable laughter. Side-splitting, tear-leaking, fumbling laughter. I have never laughed harder than in the wilderness. Not because I am happy—I don't care if I'm happy. I'm free.

Getting to this point means some sort of mild trouble has occurred, which, for the record, you should never *try* for. I'm talking about the inevitable trouble that finds you—and the silver lining that comes with it. The kind of low-level "crisis" that makes you laugh until your face hurts.

Then there's the kind of crisis without quotation marks—the kind that is still married to the Unknown, a looming, dark beast that you cannot bribe with jokes. In this book, I have tried to make backpacking seem easy, approachable, and accessible—fun even. But the truth is no adventure exists without some threat of danger. And if the danger isn't real, the adventure has no teeth. There are hundreds of ways to die in the backcountry, including dehydration, bleeding out, hypothermia, altitude sickness, infection, drowning, crush syndrome, brain damage, being masticated, and simply being outside for too long (also called "exposure," usually the result of a broken limb that prevents you from doing anything but lying down and slowly dying). The cold truth is that if you get seriously hurt or sick in the backcountry, you have options, but they are limited. Very limited.

"CPR in the wilderness is little more than a death ritual." This was one of my first lessons in wilderness medicine—that is, medicine practiced miles away from anything sterile and likely by someone who lacks an actual medical degree. I was sixteen, sitting in the front row of my classroom in Team, while my teacher Chuck explained in his scratchy, mad-professor voice that even if we successfully managed to resuscitate a person using whatever number of chest compressions and French kisses

WHAT'S IN MY WILDERNESS MEDICINE KIT

I used to carry an entire prepackaged, certified first-aid kit into the wilderness—the ones with scissors and gloves and those tin foil blankets and everything. But I got tired of digging through an ocean of custom adhesive bandage shapes and moist towelettes every time I was (mildly) hurt, when all I ever seemed to need was ibuprofen and a roll of tape.

This is everything I take in my med kit now, and so far, it's all I've ever needed:

- **Medication** (for me that means ibuprofen, Imodium, and Benadryl, in a baggie with their expiration dates written on the front)
- **Tweezers** (for ticks and splinters)
- **Gauze** in a sterile package
- **A compression bandage**
- **A few adhesive bandages** (for nostalgia's sake, I guess)
- **A bottle of iodine** (both as backup water treatment and to clean wounds)
- **A small needle and a bit of thread** (great for patching holes in your clothes too)
- **A water filter syringe,** which can double as an irrigation syringe
- **Gaffer tape** (which is usually floating around somewhere else, performing seventy other functions)

was recommended circa 2004, they weren't exactly going anywhere with that chest full of cracked ribs you just gave them.

Lessons like this one are probably why I panic so easily the minute something goes off plan in the backcountry. I have very little faith that things are going to work out in my favor in general, and out here the stakes are much higher than when I'm within driving distance of an urgent care clinic.

This isn't to say wilderness medicine is useless—far from it. You should absolutely attend a live education session with the National Outdoor Leadership School (NOLS), or at least read through a recently published book on wilderness medicine, before you head out into the backcountry. I can't offer you such advice here, because I'm too afraid of being legally liable for your death when you, say, follow my instructions on how to irrigate a gash with your water filter. I strongly suggest you take a class from an actual professional. They're useful for far more than life-or-death scenarios. I use the knowledge I've gained from such courses every single time I go into the backcountry. Whether it's knowing how to splint a broken limb with tree branches, treat small scrapes before they get infected, or prevent trench foot, this wilderness medicine stuff comes in handy well before it saves your life.

I'd like to tell you some truly exotic wilderness medicine tale about how I survived a shattered femur or got half-eaten by a bear and dragged myself on my belly for forty miles to safety. Most exciting wilderness emergency stories have plots like this—especially if they are told through the cold, forensic lens of a rescue team putting together the evidence of what happened to the deceased. The majority of wilderness medicine stories told by the living, however, center less on near-death experiences, and more on the contemplation of the hand-wringing, leg-trembling, lip-biting question: "OK, but . . . how fucked am I, really?"

Barring, of course, the kind of obvious emergency where you are bleeding out of your carotid artery or actively being eaten by a wolverine, I've found that crisis in the backcountry is not so much an event as a state of mind. In other words, one of the most important lessons of wilderness medicine is learning how to differentiate between when you're OK and just need to tough it out, and when you're at risk of dying—but still have time to be saved.

JEANNE, IRINA, AND I SPENT two days trying to find the trail we walked away from on Puyehue. Two days of wandering over red, white, and gray Martian hills, dotted with glowing pockets of green minerals and towers of neon sulfur, set to the distant soundtrack of *pop, pop, pop*s as fumaroles burst into the sky. We used the obsidian glacier, the cone of the volcano top, the sun, and the tree line to orient ourselves roughly on the map. But no matter what we did, we couldn't ever seem to find the trail. We also kept running into handfuls of pure white butterflies that would hover around us, fluttering their small angel wings as if in encouragement. "This must be a sign," we would think, with the starry eyes of teenage girls raised on Greek myths and Disney movies. We would follow them for a while, but they only seemed to lead us to house-size bowls of bright-green and egg-yolk-yellow minerals, steaming and hissing at us like fetal sarlacc pits.

We did find, serendipitously, a road at the edge of the tree line near the obsidian glacier, as well as a clear, flowing creek. The sight of this made my chest unlock in relief. But, as where the road led to was beyond the coverage of our map, we did not immediately leap for joy. We had been explicitly told, with some seriousness by the park rangers, not to take any unfamiliar roads we saw up on this mountain, and that we must stay on the trail around the volcano no matter what. Still, the road was covered in tire marks, which meant it led back to civilization. Just not necessarily friends. We filed it under plan B.

I still had my cell phone in my backpack, turned off to save the battery. I told myself I could always turn it on and call for help, that I was merely a few comforting presses of a button away from a red and white helicopter picking me up and getting me out of here—I was simply *choosing* not to summon it. Somehow, I had gotten it in my head that an emergency airlift would cost $10,000. I don't know where I first heard this figure, but I

YOU CAN TEXT IN THE BACKCOUNTRY. HOORAY.

Satellite messengers allow you to not only send an SOS signal that will connect you with emergency services but also to send text messages to your friends and loved ones while on the trail. A number of companies (including Garmin and SPOT) sell satellite messengers, in a variety of sizes.

If opening yourself up to your friends and family's text chains about the latest spilled tea in your friends group or how big a hairball your cat just coughed up on the floor while you're trying to spend some quality time in nature sounds unappealing, don't despair. It's possible to have the security of a satellite messenger without the hairball play-by-play by opting to carry a **personal locator beacon**, a.k.a. the PLB. Instead of screens, these are essentially plastic bricks that house a solitary button. When it's pressed, a signal is sent to a global satellite system, which will then alert a network of rescue agencies that you are in distress. Who ends up coming (and when exactly) will be a mystery until they arrive. But at least no one can guilt trip you for not texting them back while you were trying to run away from the world.

Personal locator beacon versus satellite messenger

seemed to remember it from a past wilderness medicine course. So every day we couldn't find the trail, I asked myself, "Are you lost? Or are you $10,000 lost?" And every time the answer was "no," I kept walking. We had food and water and each other. For these reasons alone, Jeanne was convinced nothing was wrong at all and, in many ways, she was right. The truth is, I was too afraid to turn on my phone and risk discovering that I had no emergency cell service; that the help line I could call—the salvation to which I thought I was saying "oh, no thanks" every day—didn't actually exist. I wasn't sure that knowledge was something I could ever recover from. So I kept Schrödinger's bars of service safely in the box. It was doing me more favors there.

In reality, I probably wouldn't have been able to call for help, because cell phones generally don't have service in the backcountry, especially not on active volcanoes. In most parts of the world, the only way to reliably send a backcountry digital distress signal to a search and rescue team is to carry a satellite messenger or a personal locator beacon.

Jeanne and I never carried a beacon, so I didn't have one of these with me on the volcano. My emergency plan on Puyehue was the same one it had always been: I would turn to Jeanne at the start of whatever trip we were on and say, "OK, so if one of us passes out, the still-awake person leaves the food and water with the faintee, pins a note to their chest, and

THE TEN ESSENTIALS

The point of the Ten Essentials, originated by The Mountaineers, has always been to answer two basic questions: Can you prevent emergencies and respond positively should one occur (items 1–5)? And can you safely spend a night—or more—outside (items 6–10)? These are categories rather than specific items; what you take from each category is largely up to you. However, know that a lost, scared version of your future self sends their thanks for choosing well.

1. **Navigation:** map, compass, altimeter, GPS device, and personal locator beacon (PLB) or satellite messenger
2. **Headlamp:** plus extra batteries
3. **Sun protection:** sunscreen, sunglasses, hat, etc.
4. **First aid:** bandages; skin closures; gauze pads and dressings; roller bandage or wrap; tape; antiseptic; blister prevention and treatment supplies; nitrile gloves; tweezers; needle; nonprescription painkillers; anti-inflammatory, anti-diarrheal, and antihistamine tablets; topical antibiotic; and any important personal prescriptions, including an EpiPen if you are allergic to bee or hornet venom
5. **Knife**
6. **Fire and firestarter**
7. **Shelter:** a light emergency bivvy at a minimum
8. **Extra food:** snacks that could sustain you beyond the period of time you expect to be out
9. **Extra water:** or a small water filter, if you will be traveling through an area with reliable water sources
10. **Warmth:** a layer of warm clothing for when the temperature drops

runs for help. Right?" "Right," she'd respond. It was a perfect system, especially considering we'd never had to execute it.

So what really qualifies as a backcountry emergency? When do you know it's time to press the magic button that—assuming it works—summons benevolent Big Brother to whisk you off to safety? Moreover, what happens after you do?

"You feel disappointed, in a way—guilty," my former co-worker Andrew told me, when I asked him about this years later. Andrew is an affable Canadian engineer whose idea of a good time is as follows: drive up to 7,000 feet in the Sierra Nevada in February, sleep on the ground outside of his car, wake up, high-five a bear, hike to the top of a hill, and ski eighty miles per hour down any route that "looks good."[40] So when Andrew fractured his tibia on some hard ice in Jasper National Park in Canada, he wasn't so injured that he and his friends didn't first try to combine their resources and craft a way to get him off the mountain (imagine a "Martha Stewart ski emergency challenge"). But, when none of the makeshift sled and pulley ideas would work, and with the sun starting to set, it became increasingly obvious that they were fucked. (Andrew did not use the word "fucked," but in my opinion, if you are experiencing the inability to self-extract, you are fucked.)

"There's a moment where you think, 'OK, I'm going to use this little magic wand I've carried for ten years . . . what's going to happen?' Then you push it and nothing happens but a little light starts to flash. It's almost like you were expecting an explosion."

He and his friends waited as the sun went down over the ice field. "That's actually when the pain started. After you've accepted what you need to do and you're not trying to solve anything anymore. You're just waiting. And then you feel guilty, embarrassed . . . you're the team that needed to wave the little white flag. There's a lot of self-doubt."

After a few tense hours, a helicopter came to extract him. He later received the phone number of a member of the rescue team and found the courage to ask, "In your honest opinion, do you think we made the right decision? Should we have attempted to self-extract, or did we use your resources correctly?"

"You did the right thing," replied the rescuer. "It was getting dark; you had a long ride back to your cabin. You were completely unable to stand, and it's unlikely your friends would have been able to carry you without getting injured themselves."

Most life-or-death situations in the wilderness come in one of two flavors: The first one is where you don't doubt you need help—and you will likely already be dead by the time anyone comes to help you. The other

---

40. He also finds the term "adrenaline junkie" offensive.

kind is where you're conscious, sober, and self-aware enough to think, "Do I need this? Do I deserve this? Am I weak for even thinking about this?"

This decision requires looking beyond pride, beyond plans, beyond the blind and joyful masochism that characterizes the entire endeavor of backpacking. The definition of a backcountry emergency is that you cannot get out on your own anymore. When that happens, you need to forgive yourself and push the help button. Push it while you still can.

IRINA, JEANNE, AND I DID not need to be airlifted out of Puyehue. We were lost. We were running out of food. But we had not "exhausted all options of self-extraction," as our theoretical search-and-rescue report might have said.

On our last day of food, we decided to take the forbidden dirt road down into the jungle. We had searched for three days for our trail—any trail—and come up empty. It was time to enter another unknown, but at least one that probably led to more food, and fewer asshole butterflies leading us to sulfur pits.

The road was a wide river of dust covered in tire marks. It meandered through wet, glistening green leaves and past small lakes, abandoned forestry operations, and even an empty cabin. These signs of human life were exciting, if a touch creepy, after three days of being effectively on the moon.

At one point the road split and, after a lengthy debate, we chose a direction to turn. It turned out to be wrong—we hit a dead end after two miles. So we backtracked to the last junction, me fuming and muttering under a bitter cloud of knowledge that we had wasted four miles. We walked until the road turned into a trail and then back to a road. We walked until we ran out of trail mix. We walked until we fell down on the road, and then got up again and walked some more. No one was keeping track, but in retrospect we probably walked around thirty miles.

Finally, as the glow of sunset began to warm the horizon, we saw a town at the bottom of the hill. A village, really, but it was clearly the end of the road. We cheered, rejuvenated with hope, and burst down the remaining switchbacks, eventually tumbling into the back edge of a cow ranch, panting, bleary, and trembling all over. We looked up to see where we had landed. Three farmhands stood in the distance, staring at us like we were ghosts.

We had found a way home completely off map, without injury, and without calling anyone for help. My guess is I had the swagger of a rogue at level twenty with the boss battle completed. Hero Protagonist saves the day; let's see those end credits.

The farmhands, however, did not think we were cute, or heroic, or any other adjective shared by She-Ra. In fact, they did not think we were in any need of help whatsoever.

Instead they said, with some urgency, "You need to get out of here. You need to get out of here, right now."

Aching in every muscle, we agreed: "We'll gladly get out of here. Could you give us a lift to the highway?"

"No. You need to get out of here."

"We will happily, if you give us a lift to the highway."

"You aren't allowed in the cars. You can walk."

"We came from the top of the volcano. Please. We've been walking all day and the sun is setting. We can't walk anymore."

"I walk up to the volcano every morning, girls. It's not hard."

A silence. We teetered in our boots, like dry tree trunks creaking in the breeze. Someone will always think your bestseller survival story is nothing more than their Tuesday morning workout. Eventually, Irina convinced them to pile us into a car. A nervous farmer drove us quickly toward the road, while explaining that this was the ex-dictator's land, and no one else was allowed on it.

He dumped us off at the mouth of the farm, kicking up dust as the truck drove away again. We stuck out our thumbs, and by the grace of fate, a mini-van pulled over and gave us a ride. We thanked the family profusely, and asked if they knew of any cafés that were still open—a longshot considering the town was barely more than a cluster of farms and it was apparently Sunday. They dropped us off in front of a café (really a house) with a shut door and wished us luck.

After knocking, we tentatively cracked the door open and ventured a "hello?" A kind, grandmotherly woman turned around, took one look at us, and gasped in horror. She strode forward, asking a thousand questions in

Spanish, put our cheeks in her hands and cooed at us as we whimpered and sniffled and offered her all the money in our wallets for approximately 708 empanadas. We were finally safe. We were done.

Days later, on the way out of the valley of the volcano, we visited the ranger station—the same one we had visited before heading up to the summit. There, we discovered that our map-reading skills, which we had doubted over and over again on the mountain, were perfectly fine. The trail we'd been looking for so desperately no longer existed: it had been erased in a major volcanic eruption a few years earlier.

The park had sold us an outdated map.

EPILOGUE

Despite all the safety lessons, packing advice, and navigation tips, the one thing no one ever prepared me for during all my backpacking training was what happens when you come home.

"Culture shock" is a term white people like to use to describe their discomfort after spending two-plus weeks teaching English without any qualifications in a developing nation.[41] In truth, however, culture shock describes any situation where you are taken out of your typical surroundings and put somewhere else, where even the most mundane tasks—like buying food, drinking water, sitting down, reading signs, and knowing where toilets are and how they work—are different. Everything has to be relearned, as if you were a baby. Except you're an adult, so not only do you not know how to ask for help, but no one realizes you need it. You end up carrying around a constant low-level feeling of powerlessness, equal parts frustrated and afraid that you can't do simple things like light a stove or wash your clothes. It often manifests in bouts of sobbing. It is awful.

It's not hard to imagine having culture shock out in the wilderness. You have to cook your food differently, relieve yourself differently, sleep differently . . . everything is so foreign compared to what you do at home on autopilot. This is a huge part of why I, and so many people I know, tend to get a little depressed on their first night out. You're essentially a lost, parentless

---

41. I get to make this jab because I've done this.

baby, surrounded by helpful tools you don't feel confident using. The normal background rhythms of your life are shattered, and it's normal to start desperately craving something—anything—familiar.

However, what's weirder is the culture shock you get when you return home to everything you're used to. Or were used to. On the trail, what is foreign eventually becomes familiar. I mean, it takes a second. You don't become Tom Hanks in *Castaway* over the span of a weekend. But if you go out for a week? More? You might not learn how to spear your own fish, but you'll build a new daily rhythm of packing up your gear, walking, snacking, cooking dinner, stretching, setting up your camp, and sleeping sweetly in your bag. Your new, unfamiliar tools become second limbs. Your new life becomes normal, soothing, even enjoyable. Then you come home, and this rhythm gets shattered again.

My first backpacking trip with Team was over twelve days long. On the car ride back, we stopped at a drive-in and finally got our hands on the fresh, gigantic cheeseburgers and chilled, creamy milkshakes we'd all been dreaming about in the dust of the trail. But for some reason, once in my mouth, these celebration treats tasted completely unremarkable. Halfway through, I think I even realized what I actually wanted was a salad; I had been eating processed food for twelve days, but I couldn't remember the last time I had romaine or an apple. My mother was a health nut who never let my sisters and me eat fast food. Cheeseburgers had been a special treat my whole life. My lack of desire to eat this forbidden meal practically had me staring at my own hands in wonder.

After a long, hot car ride, I finally arrived at the doorstep of my house. I was so ready to be home. But upon opening the door, it was as if the 75-watt light bulbs in the hallway were suddenly irradiating me. Everything looked familiar, but like I was outside of it, watching myself move through a scene on TV. I walked upstairs, feeling like a bug under a microscope, toward something I had dreamt most of all about on the trail: an extra-hot, extra-long, ridiculously soapy shower. So I was confused when I stepped under the hot water and realized it didn't feel as good as I'd imagined. I didn't hate it. But I seemed to get more comfort pining for it in the backcountry than in actually experiencing it at home. The water out there felt brutal and cold; the water here felt cloying and unnecessary. I scrubbed my fingernails and watched the Sierra Nevada dust on my body collide with soap bubbles and swirl down the drain. I stared at my razor—it had been a week since I shaved my legs. I picked it up, and then put it back down. What was the point? Who was I shaving for? Did I used to think leg hair was gross? I looked down at my prickly legs. I wasn't dead. Just fuzzy.

I stepped out of the shower into a fog of sweet, artificial floral scents. Wiping down the mirror, I looked at myself. (When is the last time you went over a week without seeing what you looked like?)

I saw a familiar face, but it wasn't quite how I remembered it. It was too tan for a normal October. It had a few pimples and scars I didn't remember having before. It looked a little concerned. It also had the same flaws, which was the worst part. I suppose I was expecting all the hard physical labor to have turned me into Kate Upton. It certainly felt like I had earned that. Instead, everything looked the same. I rotated in the front of the mirror. OK, everything was the same except I appeared to have swapped butts with Jennifer Lopez. Hmm, not bad.

I went into my bedroom and put on my pajamas. Clean clothing. I took a deep breath. Finally, something did feel good. I looked over the contents of my room. So many things—I forgot I had this much stuff. Why did I have so much stuff? My eyes eventually settled on the corner of my room where my stereo sat. I walked over and turned it on.

My stereo transformed into a show of lights and sounds. Music exploded out of the speakers: vocals, synthesizers, drums, and bass raced to life in perfect, familiar formations. I stared at it like I had just discovered fire. I actually knelt down in front of it and just listened. I became overwhelmed with the feeling that "this is magic. I am living in a time of actual magic." I had never been more grateful. What did people do before the radio? "Oh my god. I am a princess. A rotten, spoiled princess."

Later in the week, I would go inside a Safeway, walk toward the dairy aisle, and suddenly start crying in front of the yogurt. I would go out every night for a week and stare at the stars, not wanting to go inside, because my ceiling felt like the lid of a coffin. I wasn't wild. I was still far from wild. But I wasn't quite tame anymore either.

Most of these effects were temporary. I went back to shaving my legs and wearing makeup and I very, very much enjoy sleeping in a clean bed.

But, luckily, some of the effects lasted longer: gratitude for things I once considered normal, patience with uncertainty, and a sense of humor about the subjective way we live, survive, and take care of ourselves.

However, for all of the gratitude, it should be noted I was not exactly a peach on this first trip. I was ravaged with back pain, exhausted most days, and probably complained constantly. But on the last day, I was sitting on the edge of a glittering silver lake in a forest of slender, white-armed aspen with leaves that quaked like flecks of gold in the air. I was still, and in the stillness, both panicking and internally torn. I turned to Linn, one of the leaders on our trip, and said, "I don't want to go. I don't feel good. Everything hurts. But I don't want to go. It's weird. I don't know what to do."

She smiled at me. "It's not weird."

I held back tears. Why was I holding back tears? I had no words to articulate how I was feeling.

She seemed unperturbed. "Do you remember the first night? The moonrise over the rocks over there?"

I nodded. On our first evening, we camped on a tremendous granite outcrop. Night fell, and then immediately a round, sunbright face began to rise in an ever-widening smile over the jagged spikes of granite, casting the world in bright, cold silver—a Greek myth come to life. It was the biggest moon I had ever seen.

"That's still going to be here. Night after night. No matter where you go, or what you do, you can know that every night, the moon will be here, rising over the cliffs."

Some nights, this is still the only thought that gets me to sleep.

ACKNOWLEDGMENTS

Writing a book is a bit like figuring your way out of a dungeon. For any chance of success, you'll need to acquire teammates and helpful guides along the way. My first thanks goes to Joanna Robinson, who found me shaking at the entryway, placed a torch into my hand, and said, "This way." Which led me to Danielle Svetcov, a woman so snappy and brilliant I am still shocked she allowed me to trick her into thinking this book was a good idea, much less go on to convince Kate Rogers at Mountaineers Books too. Kate made my wildest dreams come true, and then connected me to Janice Lee, Laura Shauger, and Laura Lancaster, three women who saved me from the monsters in my writing more than once.

But at a certain point, I realized I wasn't walking alone in the darkness at all. The good people of The Naming Convention—Meg Elison, Shannon Chamberlain, Lauren Parker, and Louis Evans—gave me brilliant advice and ideas at every new junction of this manuscript.

And of course there are the spirits and memories I invoked along the way: Chuck Ford, legendary Papa of the Team program; Patchen Homitz, who taught me how to stay alive in the wilderness and never stopped encouraging my writing; Gwendolyn Grote, who taught me how to "go deeper" in my subtext; my mother, my fearless sisters Jacole and Kim, and all twenty-three members of the Team program, class of 2005.

And of course there's the magnificent Latasha Dunston, who took my hair-brained ideas about shoes in boxing arenas and passive-aggressive hair dryers and turned them into brilliant, sparkling gold. Thank you for breathing visual life into this book.

Above all, I would be nowhere without Jeanne Johnson, the Frodo to my Sam, who has been drafting this book with me for fifteen years.

Finally, there is the light at the end of the tunnel, the person who has watched me laugh and cry through the daily ins and outs of this entire process: Justin Castilla, you are the backpacking partner I begged the universe for. I promise to repay you for your toenails.

RESOURCES

ROUTES AND FORECASTS

Backpacker magazine, www.backpacker.com: Monthly magazine featuring trip ideas, backpacking skills, gear reviews, and more

Bearfoot Theory, www.bearfoottheory.com: Website featuring backpacking trip ideas, skills, and more

CalTopo, www.caltopo.com: Free mapping website with USGS topo map database layer and the option for layering other public lands data on maps; excellent resource for both PDF and printed maps

Gaia GPS, www.gaiagps.com: Smartphone app available on both Apple and Android devices offering location services and topographic maps, with the option of downloading map files

Hiking Project, www.hikingproject.com: Crowd-sourced hiking guide with photos and detailed elevation data

InciWeb, www.inciweb.com: Interagency information management system that collects news and updates for wildfires, prescribed burns, floods, hurricanes, and more

Mountain Forecast, www.mountain-forecast.com: Dedicated mountain weather forecasts for summits around the world

OpenCycleMap, www.opencyclemap.org: Global cycling map based on data from the OpenStreetMap project

USGS topographic maps, https://store.usgs.gov/map-locator: Map locator page enables hikers to figure out which paper USGS maps cover their trips; can also download PDF maps

ViewRanger, viewranger.com: Library of crowdsourced hiking routes with a variety of maps; smartphone app available

HIKING GROUPS

Hike it Baby, www.hikeitbaby.com: Hiking group that connects families with young children to each other for outings

Unlikely Hikers, jennybruso.com/unlikelyhikers/: Diverse, anti-racist, body-liberating outdoor community featuring the underrepresented outdoorsperson

Women Who Hike, www.womenwhohike.com: Worldwide organization that empowers women on and off the trail

NATIONAL WILDERNESS MEDICINE TRAINING COURSES

National Outdoor Leadership School, www.nols.edu: Nonprofit global wilderness school based in Lander, Wyoming

Wilderness Medical Associates International, www.wildmed.com: Worldwide educational organization focused on the development of remote and practical medicine

ABOUT THE AUTHOR & ILLUSTRATOR

Diana Helmuth spent much of high school taping magazine cut-outs of wilderness landscapes onto her bedroom wall where most people put band posters. She graduated from UC Berkeley and went on to moonlight in Silicon Valley's startup land as a user researcher, marketer, and operations manager. Her freelance work can be found in various travel books and Bay Area culture magazines. In addition to writing, she helps produce the occasional podcast. She lives in Oakland with an erratically planted garden, a lumberjack, and two spoiled cats.

An illustrator and painter, **Latasha Dunston** earned a BFA from Virginia Commonwealth University School of the Arts. Her clients include Otterbox, *Range Magazine*, Craghoppers, SNEWs, and the Denver Art Museum. Dunston is based in Denver.

MOUNTAINEERS BOOKS including its two imprints, Skipstone and Braided River, is a leading publisher of quality outdoor recreation, sustainability, and conservation titles. As a 501(c)(3) nonprofit, we are committed to supporting the environmental and educational goals of our organization by providing expert information on human-powered adventure, sustainable practices at home and on the trail, and preservation of wilderness.

Our publications are made possible through the generosity of donors, and through sales of 700 titles on outdoor recreation, sustainable lifestyle, and conservation. To donate, purchase books, or learn more, visit us online:

MOUNTAINEERS BOOKS

1001 SW Klickitat Way, Suite 201 • Seattle, WA 98134
800-553-4453 • mbooks@mountaineersbooks.org • www.mountaineersbooks.org

An independent nonprofit publisher since 1960

Mountaineers Books is proud to support the Leave No Trace Center for Outdoor Ethics, whose mission is to promote and inspire responsible outdoor recreation through education, research, and partnerships. The Leave No Trace program is focused specifically on human-powered (nonmotorized) recreation. For more information, visit www.lnt.org.

YOU MAY ALSO LIKE